"Brilliant, visionary, and essential, this is one of the wisest and most important Buddhist-inspired books of our era. Joanna Macy is a master, and her powerful, heart-centered work is a blessing, showing us how to transform ourselves and the world."

—JACK KORNFIELD, AUTHOR OF *A PATH WITH HEART*

"With this modernized offer of *World as Lover, World as Self*, Joanna Macy unveils an ancient set of roots for our work to transform the future. As we learn to wield the weapons of compassion and insight to fulfill our destiny, Macy weaves the spirit work of Buddhism into our community and activism work, helping us grasp where we are in the Great Turning."

—ADRIENNE MAREE BROWN, AUTHOR OF *EMERGENT STRATEGY*

"As a son of West African soils, I know how to recognize an elder's voice. Let me tell you: an elder's voice cracks with a humble vitality more compelling than truth, more urgent than caution, more liberating than prediction. Joanna Macy writes with that familiar lilt of prophecy—the stern kind of speaking that kindles spaces for new kinds of movements, comings and goings previously thought impossible. The kind of writing that softly bewilders, emancipating us from our significatory prisons and their exhausting anxieties. From within the spinning gyres of civilizational impasses, in a pandemic-inflected time when the world seems to be kicking back against the presumptuousness of human centrality, when everything seems to be collapsing, Joanna Macy sings a song to urge us not to run away, not to shrink away from these material irruptions, but to open our hearts and anchor our bodies to a world so sensuously alive that it could only be described as a lover. May we never outgrow our elders."

—BAYO AKOMOLAFE, PHD, AUTHOR OF *THESE WILDS BEYOND OUR FENCES*

"I think this book will need to be reissued every few years, as long as there are still people on the planet trying to figure out how to make it all somehow come out okay. It's as powerful as it ever was—maybe more so."

—BILL MCKIBBEN, COFOUNDER OF 350.ORG

"*World as Lover, World as Self* is essential reading. The new, thoroughly reimagined thirtieth anniversary edition, however, takes essential to another level. This new edition weaves together Macy's decades-old wisdom with fresh insights that speak directly to our troubled times. As Macy astutely notes, we have "entered the bardo" a space between worlds where the line between the Great Unraveling and the Great Turning is razor-thin. What better guide could we have in this moment than Macy herself, who draws deeply from the three wells of engaged Buddhism, deep ecology, and systems theory to bring us clear-eyed visions of how to build a sustainable society? Offering both insights for scholars and guidelines for activists, Macy teaches us to ground in gratitude, acknowledge pain, see with new eyes and commit to doing the transformative work to which each of us is distinctly called."

—REBECCA KNEALE GOULD, ENVIRONMENTAL STUDIES, MIDDLEBURY COLLEGE

"Thirty years after its original publication, the wisdom in these pages remains timeless and universal while the message has become even more pressing. As we face increasing catastrophes due to the climate crisis, Joanna's teachings become even more critical. We need this book now more than ever."

—KAZU HAGA, AUTHOR OF *HEALING RESISTANCE*

"Thank you! It's such a blessing to have Joanna's timeless handbook for the Buddhist social activist available in an updated form. Here she coaches us in the broad view of interdependence, the skillful actions for right now, and the visionary future of compassionate engagement for the suffering planet."

—ACHARYA JUDITH SIMMER-BROWN, NAROPA UNIVERSITY, AND AUTHOR OF *DAKINI'S WARM BREATH*

"What a treasure to have Joanna Macy's clear and compassionate thinking between the covers of a book. She is no armchair traveler in the realms of Buddhist philosophy and social commitment. These pages are worldly wise with experience, and earth wise with care. What a brilliant teacher this is, and what a wonderful pleasure the learning."

—SUSAN GRIFFIN, AUTHOR OF *WOMEN AND NATURE*

"Joanna Macy's life radiates out to touch and enliven every cell within our larger, spherical Body. By giving herself with such abandon to the very presence of the present moment, Joanna's tears and her joy—like those of any genuine bodhisattva—reverberate backward and forward through time to nourish all moments within the broad life of the breathing Earth."

—DAVID ABRAM, AUTHOR OF *THE SPELL OF THE SENSUOUS*

"*World as Lover, World as Self* is a lamentation, a praise song, and a map. Whoever dares, as Joanna Macy does, to love so deeply must be a descendent of the Mother of All Buddhas. In these darkest times, this book is an inextinguishable light."

—DEENA METZGER, AUTHOR OF *WRITING FOR YOUR LIFE*

ALSO BY JOANNA MACY

Coming Back to Life: The Updated Guide to the Work That Reconnects (with Molly Brown)

Active Hope: How to Face the Mess We're in without Going Crazy (with Chris Johnstone)

Pass It On: Five Stories That Can Change the World (with Norbert Gahbler)

Widening Circles: A Memoir

Mutual Causality in Buddhism and General Systems Theory: The Dharma of Natural Systems

Thinking Like a Mountain: Towards a Council of All Beings (with John Seed, Pat Fleming, and Arne Naess)

Dharma and Development: Religion as Resource in the Sarvodaya Self-Help Movement

Despair and Personal Power in the Nuclear Age

Despairwork

* * *

Translations of Rainer Maria Rilke, with Anita Barrows

Rilke's Letters to a Young Poet: A New Translation and Commentary

In Praise of Mortality: Selections from Rainer Maria Rilke's Duino Elegies and Sonnets to Orpheus

A Year with Rilke: Daily Readings from the Best of Rainer Maria Rilke

Rilke's Book of Hours: Love Poems to God

* * *

Also see A Wild Love for the World: Joanna Macy and the Work of Our Time (edited by Stephanie Kaza)

WORLD AS LOVER, WORLD AS SELF

Courage for Global Justice and Planetary Awakening

30TH ANNIVERSARY EDITION

Joanna Macy

Edited by Stephanie Kaza

PARALLAX PRESS
BERKELEY, CALIFORNIA

PARALLAX PRESS

2236B Sixth Street
Berkeley, California 94710
parallax.org

Parallax Press is the publishing division of Plum Village Community
of Engaged Buddhism, Inc.
Printed in Canada

Edited by Stephanie Kaza
Cover photograph © Jānis Grodums
Cover and text design by Katie Eberle
Composition by Happenstance Type-O-Rama

Printed on 100 percent post-consumer waste recycled paper

Library of Congress Cataloging-in-Publication Data
Names: Macy, Joanna, 1929– author. | Kaza, Stephanie, editor.
Title: World as lover, world as self : 30th anniversary edition / Joanna Macy ;
edited by Stephanie Kaza.
Description: Third edition. | Berkeley : Parallax Press, 2021. | Includes
bibliographical references. | Summary: "Draws on a lifetime of wisdom to
offer a re-focus on the natural world, where readers can find the strength
and spiritual nourishment to envision a new future for humanity built on a
sustainable relationship with the earth"—Provided by publisher.
Identifiers: LCCN 2021000922 (print) | LCCN 2021000923 (ebook) | ISBN
9781946764843 (trade paperback) | ISBN 9781946764850 (ebook)
Subjects: LCSH: Buddhism—Social aspects. | Human ecology—Philosophy.
| System theory.
Classification: LCC BQ4570.S6 M33 2021 (print) | LCC BQ4570.S6 (ebook)
| DDC 294.3/42—dc23
LC record available at https://lccn.loc.gov/2021000922
LC ebook record available at https://lccn.loc.gov/2021000923

2 3 4 5 / 25 24 23 22

I should not like to have the bodhisattva think this kind of work hard to achieve and hard to plan out. If he did, there are beings beyond calculation, and he will not be able to benefit them. Let him on the contrary consider the work easy and pleasant, thinking they were all his mother and father and children, for this is the way to benefit all beings whose number is beyond calculation.

—THE PERFECTION OF WISDOM IN 8,000 LINES

A NOTE ON USAGE

This book includes many traditional Buddhist terms. For the most part, these terms are used in Pali, the language in which the earliest Buddhist scriptures were recorded. However, for the following terms and proper names, the Sanskrit equivalents are used, as these are already familiar to many Western readers: atman, bodhisattva, chakra, dharma, karma, nirvana, prajña, Sariputra, Siddhartha Gautama, and sutra. Most foreign terms are italicized the first time they appear in the text. Diacritical marks have been omitted. Textual references appear at the end of the book.

CONTENTS

Forewords

THICH NHAT HANH, 1991 xi
STEPHANIE KAZA, 2007 xiii
REVEREND JOAN JIKO HALIFAX, 2021 xvi

Prologue: Entering the Bardo

. . . . xix

I. Finding Our Bearings

1. WORLD AS LOVER, WORLD AS SELF 3
2. GROUNDING IN GRATITUDE 19
3. THE GATEWAY OF DESPAIR 33
4. WISDOM AND ACTION 47

II. Food for the Mind

5. THE WHEEL OF INTERBEING 61
6. THE CO-ARISING OF KNOWER AND KNOWN 75
7. KARMA: THE CO-ARISING OF DOER AND DEED . . . 85
8. THE CO-ARISING OF SELF AND SOCIETY 95
9. MOTHER OF ALL BUDDHAS 109

III. Food for the Heart

10. OPENINGS 125
11. THE GREENING OF THE SELF 133
12. FAITH, POWER, AND DEEP ECOLOGY 145
13. IN LEAGUE WITH THE BEINGS OF THE FUTURE . . 157
14. THE FULLNESS OF TIME 173

IV. *Food for the Journey*

15. THE GREAT TURNING 187
16. COLLECTIVE INTELLIGENCE:
    THE HOLONIC SHIFT 201
17. SHAMBHALA WARRIORS: A PROPHECY 209
18. COURAGE FOR THE ROAD 213

SPIRITUAL PRACTICES FOR ACTIVISTS 221
ACKNOWLEDGMENTS 243

FOR FURTHER STUDY
   Joanna Macy Life Timeline 247
   A Buddhist Glossary 253

NOTES 259
CREDITS 265
ABOUT JOANNA MACY 268

Life exists only in the present moment. Everything is in this moment—the past, the present, the future, and all beings in all places. When we throw a banana peel or a rose into the garbage, we know that it will decompose quickly and fertilize our garden. We also know that plastic bags and plastic diapers take much longer to break down, perhaps four hundred years. And we know that nuclear waste will take the longest time, a quarter of a million years.

In these pages, Joanna Macy shares her lucid understanding through a clear expression of these teachings of the Buddha. "This is, because that is." This is not, because that is not." This is like this, because that is like that." Everything exists within this present moment, and all things are interconnected. The poet Walt Whitman said, "I am large, I contain multitudes."

In the Avatamsaka Sutra, the Buddha tells us of the bodhisattva who is patted on the head simultaneously by all buddhas, bodhisattvas, and other beings. When we accomplish something crucial for our time, the entire universe congratulates and caresses us. In sharing her insights concerning today's perils and the important role each of us has both in creating these perils and in overcoming them, Joanna Macy speaks the truth with the roar of a lioness, and all beings throughout the universe are patting her head and caressing her in gratitude and appreciation.

I am honored to be able to introduce this important book. If we read Joanna's words attentively and put her proposals into practice, we may still have a chance to show our Mother Earth our love for her. Love requires understanding, and *World as Lover, World as Self* helps us understand how we can heal this interconnected, interpenetrating universe.

If we take the hand of a child and look at the small flowers that grow among the grasses, if we sit with him or her and breathe deeply and smile, listening to the birds and also to the sounds of the other children playing together, we will see that that message is exactly the same as the message of this book, and we will know that our future depends on both. Looking deeply into the present moment, we know what to do and what not to do to save our precious planet, and each other. This is real peace education. The deepest teachings of the Buddha are explained here. Let us join the buddhas and bodhisattvas in congratulating Joanna Macy by enjoying this book and by practicing the fruits of her insights.

FOREWORD
STEPHANIE KAZA, 2007

On Labor Day weekend 2006, a small band of concerned citizens took a long walk together to raise issues of climate change. They started in Robert Frost's birth place in Vermont and walked for five days with Bill McKibben to Burlington City Hall. Along the way they talked about the world they want for their children. Each day more people joined the group until a thousand people were gathered at Battery Park. One by one, the political candidates of both parties for all the major offices came up to the stage and signed our climate pledge.

All of us in that crowd knew the world was in unprecedented danger from global warming. Yet here we were, turning our despair into hope, our paralysis into action. As we engaged the impossible koan of climate change, we were planting seeds of faith and courage for the long haul. We were responding to the call to act on behalf of the larger whole, the miracle that is this earth, our home. We were taking up the activist's journey, each step moved by urgency but also fierce love.

In this revision of Joanna Macy's long-beloved volume, *World as Lover, World as Self*, we have some companion wisdom for the long journey. Joanna's teachings over the past thirty years have been foundational for many activists and citizens anxious about the deteriorating state of the planet. Year after year, the concerns have mounted—from pesticides to groundwater pollution, from factory farms to rainforest destruction. At times and in places, it has seemed the earth could not withstand the degree of assault inflicted upon it by its human inhabitants. Joanna Macy has offered visionary yet pragmatic leadership in facing the emotional pain of this assault. Her workshops around the world have galvanized thousands of people to take action. Using the powerful frameworks of systems analysis and eco-psychology, Joanna provides tools that are effective in even the most daunting situations.

But more than tools, these chapters are filled with gifts of the heart and mind. Joanna presents a way to be with seemingly impossible challenges, drawing on ancient teachings of the Buddha as well as modern views of eco-social systems. Here we find the core thinking of her doctoral research, more relevant than ever to environmental work today. She urges us to "come home again" to the world as both self and lover, to feel the way we are *actually* all connected—not in some fuzzy, mystical trance state but in the very real material exchanges of air, water, flesh, and heat. Macy invites us to experience the ecological self, each of us an expression of much larger self-organizing patterns.

As the decades have advanced, and environmental threats have multiplied rapidly, some people shrug their shoulders and give up, convinced they cannot stop the bulldozer of "progress." Joanna Macy takes the long view, investing in what she calls the Great Turning. Gazing into the future, she sees the shift to a life-sustaining society already taking place, being called forth by ordinary citizens. For her, the great work of this time is a fabulous adventure, risky on every front but completely worth the effort. In these pages you can almost hear her spunky laughter ring out. How could we not join her on this great journey toward sanity and health?

It can be all too tempting to fall into the trap of feeling sorry for ourselves. How did we ever get into this overwhelmingly complex fix? Joanna wastes no time in blame or anger, but takes the path of gratitude and grace. For her it is a grand privilege to be alive at this time, working together for this beautiful earth that has given us life. I see her now with that bright look in her eyes, gazing into the distance, hearing the prophecy of the Shambhala warrior. For Joanna this is no dream; it is a potent human reality, limited only by our own small imaginations. This vision of a sustainable future will require, as she says, a "burning patience" and a willingness to be completely present to the larger whole.

It is a personal honor to introduce this edition of Joanna's work. For me, like many others, Joanna has been an inspiration, a guide, and a friend along the way. Her wisdom and rich imagination have brought life-giving energy to concerned citizens around the world. We are fortunate indeed to have such an articulate and impassioned teacher in these demanding times. It is my abiding hope that we can continue to keep each other company as each of us takes up the next piece of the "work that reconnects."

FOREWORD
REVEREND JOAN JIKO HALIFAX, 2021

Joanna Macy begins the prologue of this compelling book with these provocative words: "We are in a space without a map." Our certainty has been challenged and has collapsed into a heap. Our social systems are under fire, as they burn our world. Our very climate is threatened and threatening. We are in a time of great churn, and Joanna proposes—radically and bravely—that this time can be a time of great turning—turning toward the possible, turning toward awakening, turning toward reality, as it is.

Joanna's prophetic voice, informed by science and Buddhism, has been heard through these past decades as an awakening bell for thousands of people across the planet. She was born just before the Wall Street crash of September 1929 and lived through the Great Depression that sent much of the world into a time of grinding privation, a time that both nourished the roots of her dedication to face the truth of suffering and generated her commitment to the great task of ending suffering in ourselves and in our world.

Joanna is known to many as a dedicated climate activist, a caring Buddhist, a scholar of general systems theory, a deep ecologist, and a poet and lover. Yet, these designations barely begin to describe her. When you meet Joanna, you realize you are meeting a force of nature, a person of extraordinary compassion, a person who holds nothing back, whose "strong back, soft front" make her a tuning fork for the ages.

I met Joanna forty years ago and have followed her work of personal and global transformation with respect and awe. I realized on first encountering her that this was a person whose capacity to *become the world* and to see the outcomes of cause and effect, to sense into the suffering of others—including animal species and forests and our very atmosphere—was preternatural. Her ability to embody the experience of other beings and awaken that capacity in others can set a person's teeth on edge as they feel defenses dropping away, the weight of pretenses shrinking, and the space of courage and love opening, like ice heaving and thawing, or the wild flap of raven's wings at the end of winter.

At the beginning of her book, Joanna speaks unsparingly of the first Noble Truth of Suffering. She reminds us of the grief we are experiencing at this time from the depletion of life-giving topsoil to the terrifying toxicity caused by nuclear disasters, big and small. She calls out the Sixth Extinction that we are all facing at this time, as species after species vanishes into the maw of history. She urges us not to turn away from the truth of suffering, but rather to feel it, to bear witness to it, to be one with it. She calls us out of our houses, out of the safety of our minds, out of the crevasses of fear that we have shrunk into, and into the threatening and beautiful expansiveness that unfolds when we feel the pain of other beings and feel the sickness of our earth and her species and feel the possibility of healing for all.

Joanna herself has known the despair of which she speaks. Her urgings do not shame, but they awaken and heal those who heed her and heed themselves, as they discover the wounds of aversion, neglect, and greed that have powered the destruction of our earth.

Joanna's insight into causality and interdependent co-arising challenges Western notions of the self. "Is there a separate self?" she asks. She is emphatic that there is *no* separate self: self and other are one. From this radical perspective, Joanna concludes that feelings of sorrow, loss, despair, anger, and anguish reflect our true humanity and do not deprive us of who we really are, which is not separate from all beings and things. Rather these feelings liberate us into the great circle of life. From this arises an ethos of compassionate action and the realization of deep mutuality as we meet the world as self, the world as lover.

Joanna's book is brave, disturbing, and hopeful, a sacred text for the generations. I am grateful that her life has been long and generative. She has given of herself, decade after decade, in a way that has been a living example of the very ethos she calls for, an ethos of non-separation, an ethos of deep responsibility, an ethos of love and compassion.

Joanna calls us to go forth into this wounded world as peaceful warriors in order to transform the suffering of our living planet. She also calls us to "not know," something that is difficult for those of us who rely on certainty. As she reminds us: "Not knowing rivets our attention on what is happening right now. This present moment is the *only* time we can act, and the only time, after all, we can wake up." She calls us into action *now*, into awakening *now*!

PROLOGUE
ENTERING THE BARDO

We are in a space without a map. With the likelihood of economic collapse and climate catastrophe looming, it feels like we are on shifting ground, where old habits and old scenarios no longer apply. In Tibetan Buddhism, such a space or gap between known worlds is called a *bardo*. It is frightening. It is also a place of potential transformation.

As you enter the bardo, there facing you is the Buddha Akshobhya. His element is water. He is holding a mirror, for his gift is mirror wisdom, reflecting everything just as it is. And the teaching of Akshobhya's mirror is this: *Do not look away. Do not avert your gaze. Do not turn aside.* This teaching calls for radical attention and total acceptance.

For the last forty years, I've been growing a form of experiential group work called the Work That Reconnects. It is a framework for personal and social change in the face of overwhelming crises—a way of transforming despair and apathy into collaborative action. Like the mirror wisdom of Akshobhya, the Work That Reconnects helps people tell the truth about what they see and feel is happening to our world. It also helps them find the motivation, tools, and resources for taking part in our collective self-healing.

When we come together for this work, at the outset we discern three stories or versions of reality that are shaping our world so that we can see them more clearly and choose which one we want to get behind. The first narrative we identify is

"Business as Usual," by which we mean the growth economy or global corporate capitalism. We hear this marching order from virtually every voice in government, publicly traded corporations, the military, and corporate-controlled media.

The second is called the "Great Unraveling," the ongoing collapse of life forms and human structures. This is what happens when ecological, biological, and social systems are commodified by an industrial growth society or "business as usual." I like the term *unraveling*, because systems don't just fall over dead; they fray, at first slowly, then progressively lose their coherence, integrity, and memory.

The third story is the central adventure of our time: the transition to a life-sustaining society. This transition, which is well underway when we know where to look, is comparable in scope and magnitude to the Agricultural Revolution some ten thousand years ago and to the Industrial Revolution a few centuries back. Contemporary social thinkers have various names for it, such as the "ecological revolution" or "sustainability revolution;" in the Work That Reconnects we call it the Great Turning.

Simply put, our aim with this process of naming and deep recognition of what is happening to our world is to survive the first two stories and to keep bringing more and more people and resources into the third story. Through this work, we can choose what we want to put our lives behind—business as usual, the unraveling of living systems, or the creation of a life-sustaining society.

Over the last couple of years, a number of us have recognized that, given the pace of the Great Unraveling, we are heading toward economic and, indeed, civilizational collapse. Our thinking has been aided by the Deep Adaptation work of Jem Bendell, which seeks to prepare for—and live with—societal breakdown. I'd also like to acknowledge the earlier contributions in French-speaking Europe of Pablo Servigne and Raphaël Stevens, whose prescient work focuses on collapse and transition and is only just now coming out in English.

Since the present world economy has been unable to cut greenhouse gas emissions by even the slightest fraction of a degree, it now seems obvious that we cannot avoid climate catastrophe. Many of us had assumed that the Great Turning could forestall such disintegration, but now we have come to recognize the Great Turning as a process and a commitment to help us survive the breakdown of the industrial growth economy. The motivation and skills we gain by engaging in the Work That Reconnects provide the guidance, solidarity, and trust needed to make our way through this inevitable breakdown.

There are many dimensions to this work that address current psychological and spiritual issues, and I have found a significant relevance in Buddhist thought and systems science. I now think of the Great Turning as somewhat like *bodhicitta*, the intention to serve the welfare of all beings. This is the mind state of the bodhisattva—the being who, in their great compassion, delays nirvana in order to address the world's suffering. I remember my Tibetan teachers telling me that bodhicitta is like a flame in the heart, and often I can feel it there.

It seems pretty clear now who is holding up Akshobhya's mirror—it is COVID-19. The coronavirus has come upon us fast. We knew nothing of it just a short while ago. First it made us pause so we could take in what the mirror is reflecting. We've been so busy and distracted in our different versions of the rat race that we haven't been able to pay attention to our actual situation. We had to cease our rushing about in order to see who, what, and where we are.

COVID-19 reminds us that *apocalypse*, in its ancient meaning, connotes "revelation" or "unveiling." And what has it unveiled? A pandemic so contagious that it immediately revealed our failed health care system and our utter interdependence. We suddenly needed to prioritize the collective nature of our well-being. As Malcolm X put it, "When we change the 'I' for the 'We,' even Illness becomes Wellness."

The patterns of contagion then cast a spotlight on what we most need to see: nursing homes, where seniors are concentrated; the meatpacking industry, so dangerous to the crowded workers, so cruel to the animals, so costly to the climate; prisons, where millions are locked away, now becoming petri dishes of contamination; the fault lines of racial inequality in our society, now laid bare in the pandemic's disproportionate impacts on Black, Brown, and Indigenous communities. In the United States, sixty percent of those infected are African Americans, thanks to preexisting conditions fostered by inequities in health care and environmental racism.

On top of that, the killing of George Floyd has not only revealed the racism and brutality of our police culture but also aroused unparalleled protests, sweeping the country and calling for the defunding and even abolition of police departments and unions.

Globally, as well as in the United States, many of us are discovering a new solidarity in our determination to move beyond the crippling racism we've inherited. In this uprising, I am inspired by the courage, creativity, and perseverance of those engaging in public demonstrations, who are influencing many civil servants to take action—members of city councils, agencies, and even police departments. It is no wonder that the bardo represents a place where the unknown, even the inconceivable, can happen and where we who enter are profoundly changed.

When we dare to face the cruel social and ecological realities we have been accustomed to, courage is born, and powers within us are liberated to reimagine and even, perhaps one day, rebuild a world.

Do not look away. Do not avert your gaze. Do not turn aside.

PART ONE

Finding Our Bearings

ONE

WORLD AS LOVER, WORLD AS SELF

There is a Secret One inside us,
the planets in all the galaxies
pass through his hands like beads.

—KABIR

Life on our planet is in trouble. It is hard to go anywhere without being confronted by the wounding of our world, the tearing of the very fabric of life. We are assaulted by news of wildfires and hurricanes, fleeing refugees, another police murder, the climate in chaos. Our planet is sending us signals of distress that are now so continual they seem almost normal. Reports proliferate about the erosion of forests and cropland, polluted air and toxic waters, the loss of half the world's biodiversity. These are stern warning signals that we live in a world that can end, at least as a home for conscious life. This is not to say that it *will* end, but it *can* end. That very possibility changes everything for us.

There have been small groups throughout history that have proclaimed the end of the world, such as at the beginning of the first millennium CE and again during the Black Plague in Europe. These expectations arose within the context of religious faith, of a belief in a just but angry God ready to punish his wayward children. But now the prospect of collapse is spelled out in sober scientific data, not religious belief, and it is entirely devoid of transcendent meaning. I stress the unprecedented nature of our situation, because I want to inspire respect and compassion for what we are experiencing.

Internal and external forces are at work, urging us to look away from the reality of what is happening. It is easy to let ourselves get engulfed by digital distractions and mind-numbing techno-games. The use of antidepressants, substance abuse, and suicide rates, especially among young people, are dramatically on the rise. The World Health Organization reports that anxiety and depression have reached epidemic proportions due to economic and health stressors. Many of us seem to be doing everything we can to shut out awareness of the world's real plight.

To others of us, the distress of people and planet brings a near-desperate sense of urgency to do something. But the many programs, strategies, and causes that vie for our attention also bring a sense of overwhelm. It is hard to know which of the countless separate issues we should address first, and our confusion makes it hard to see their linkages and common roots.

In the face of what is happening, how do we avoid feeling overwhelmed and just giving up? Instead of turning to the diversions and demands of our consumer society, how can we stay awake to what's really going on?

Our responses to the state of things are conditioned by our felt relationship to the world, and this is seldom conscious; it is shaped by powerful archetypes. As we recognize these archetypes, we can be both liberated and emboldened to do what must be done.

Here are four such archetypes that have come down to us through the ages. They are not specific to any culture or tradition. You can find all of them in all the major religions. These are: world as battlefield, world as trap, world as lover, and world as self.

WORLD AS BATTLEFIELD

Many people view the world as battleground where good and evil are pitted against each other and forces of light struggle against the forces of darkness. This way of seeing, reinforced by centuries of living with war, can be traced back to the ancient Zoroastrians and Manichaeans. It can be persuasive, especially when we feel threatened. Such a view is very good for arousing courage, summoning up the blood, using the fiery energies of anger and militancy.

It is very good, too, for lending a sense of certainty. Whatever the score may be at the moment or whatever the tactics we're employing, there is the reassuring sense that we are fighting God's battle—and that ultimately we will win. William Irwin Thompson has called this kind of certainty, and the self-righteousness that goes with it, the "apartheid of good."

It is a powerful force in many areas of our world today, from the Middle East to relations with Russia, and it has taken hold in the United States in community-police relations, for example, or in the War on Terror, with one president's proclamation that "you're either with us or against us." When some assert an "axis of evil," the whole world becomes a battleground. In response, US military expenditures soar, accounting for half of the world's total spending on arms.

It's not just politicians who fall prey to the battlefield frame of mind. To be constantly fighting "bad guys," be they corporations or riot police, can bring citizens and grassroots activists to the point of exhaustion and hopelessness. A do-or-die militancy, combined with self-righteousness, is a recipe for burnout or, at the very least, a loss of resilience and creativity.

There are those who tell us we can join a divinely ordained battle, leading to Armageddon and the Second Coming of Christ. In this version of Christian thought, nuclear war may be the catalyst for the millennial denouement, bringing rewards to the elect who will inherit the earth, and the bomb itself can appear as an instrument of God's will. This interpretation of biblical texts has become a force in American politics, from foreign to environmental policy.

A more innocuous version of the battlefield image of the world is the one I learned from my grandparents. It is the world as a classroom or a kind of moral gymnasium, where you are put through tests to prove your mettle and shape you up, so that you can graduate to other arenas and rewards. Whether imagined as a school or battlefield, the world is a proving ground, with little worth other than that. Our immortal souls are being tested here. They count, and the world doesn't. Indeed, in today's battles for dominance or survival, the world counts for so little that it's being destroyed.

This point of view is contagious. It spreads rapidly through fear-inducing propaganda and disinformation campaigns. Viral messages on social media present people of other political persuasions as enemies. This extreme divisiveness is ripping apart the social fabric of the country and being used to justify civil war. This polarization has tremendous appeal and tenacity. It will be hard to move forward from such a destructive paradigm without first recognizing its power.

WORLD AS TRAP

The second view is the world as trap. In this view, the goal is not to engage in struggle and vanquish the foe, but to disentangle ourselves and escape from this messy world. We try to extricate ourselves and ascend to a higher, immaterial plane. This stance is based on the view of reality where mind is seen as higher than nature, and spirit is set over and above the flesh. This view encourages contempt for the material plane. It has entered the major religions of the last five thousand years, regardless of their message and metaphysics.

Many of us on spiritual paths fall for this perspective. Wanting to affirm a transcendent reality distinct from a materialistic society, we place it on a transcendent level removed from confusion and suffering. We assign the tranquility we find in spiritual practices to a haven that is aloof from our world and to which we can ascend and be safe and serene. This gets tricky, because we still have bodies and are dependent on them, however advanced we may be on the spiritual path.

Trying to escape from something that we are dependent on breeds a love-hate relationship with it. This love-hate relationship with matter permeates our culture and breeds a deep ambivalence. We want to both possess and destroy. These two impulses, craving and aversion, inflame each other in a vicious circle. In systems terms, this could be seen as a deviation-amplifying or positive feedback loop. We can see this exemplified in the skyrocketing military buildup in the United States. To

sustain our capacity to destroy, we require increasing amounts
of raw materials, and the vicious circle intensifies.

A love-hate relationship with matter reinforces the idea
that mind and spirit are separate from the natural world and
superior to it. Dichotomies arise between spirit and flesh, light
and dark, reason and emotion, male and female, sacred and pro-
fane. The desire to possess or destroy becomes easily projected
onto Earth, the feminine, "dark" emotions, and dark-skinned
people. It feeds into societal systems of oppression. We can see
our centuries of racism, colonialism, imperialism, exploitation,
enslavement, genocide and the raping of Earth and women as
tragic consequences of the belief that the world is a trap.

Many on a spiritual path, seeking to transcend all impulses
to acquire or to destroy, put great value on detachment. They
can be reluctant to engage in the hurly-burly work of social
change. They often avoid looking at the ways in which they
themselves are complicit in and benefit from systems that perpetuate privilege and oppression.

Some Buddhists seem to understand nonattachment as
freedom from the world and its fate. But the Buddha taught
nonattachment from ego, not from the world. In fact, the
Buddha was suspicious of those who tried to detach themselves
from the material realm. Referring to yogis who mortified the
flesh in order to free the spirit, the Buddha likened their efforts
to those of a dog tied by a rope to a stake in the ground. He
said that the harder they tried to free themselves from the body,
the more they would circle round and get closer to the stake,
eventually wrapping themselves around it.

Of course, even when you see the world as a trap, you can
still feel a compassionate impulse to help its suffering beings.

In that case, the personal and the political are often viewed in a sequential fashion: "I'll find peace within myself first, then I'll join actions to stop police violence." Those who are not engaged in spiritual pursuits put it differently: "I'll get my head straight first—I'll get psychoanalyzed, I'll overcome my inhibitions or neuroses or hang-ups—and *then* I'll wade into the fray." Presupposing that world and self are essentially separate, they imagine they can heal one before healing the other. This stance conveys the impression that human consciousness inhabits some haven, or locker room, independent of the collective situation—and then trots onto the playing field when it is geared up and ready.

Another hazard of this view is fear of nature, especially during these uncertain times of climate chaos. The increasing devastation wrought by hurricanes, fire storms, and sea level rise is perceived by some as the wrath of Earth. Even environmentalists can portray nature as an object of fear and loathing, as in the title of James Lovelock's book on global warming, *The Revenge of Gaia*. But if we are an inseparable part of the natural world, who is the world taking revenge upon—itself? Such a stance obscures our deepest connections and isolates us from the source of our greatest wisdom.

It is my experience that the world itself has a role to play in our spiritual liberation. Its very pressures, pains, and risks can wake us up, release us from the bonds of ego, and guide us home to our vast, true nature.

WORLD AS LOVER

In this third view, the world is experienced not as a stage set for our moral battles or a prison to escape from, but as an essential and life-giving partner. From the curve of the cosmos to the spinning of atoms, the universe engages in a dance of mutual allurement.

Hindu culture has many expressions of our erotic relationship to the world. In early Vedic hymns, the first stirrings of life are equated with the primal pulse of eros. In the beginning there was the sacred self-existent one, Prajapati. Lonely, it created the world by splitting into two so that it could copulate with itself. Pregnant with its own inner amplitude and tension, out of desire, it gave birth to all phenomena.

In this worldview, desire plays a creative, world-manifesting role. Its charge in Hinduism pulses onward into Krishna worship, where devotional songs, or *bhajans*, draw on the yearnings of body and soul. Krishna evokes these yearnings in his devotees to bring them to the bliss of union with the divine. As you sing your longing for the dewdrop sparkle of his eyes, the nectar of his lips, the blue shade of his skin, like the thunderclouds that bring the refreshment and fertility of the monsoon, the whole world takes on his beauty and the sweetness of his flesh. You feel yourself embraced in the primal play of life.

As the thirteenth-century Hindu poet Jnaneshwar sang in his "Nectar of Self-Awareness," this ecstatic play is ever-present in each single manifestation of life.

> The lover, out of boundless love,
> takes the form of the Beloved.
> What Beauty!
> Both are made of the same nectar
> and share the same food.

Out of the Supreme Love
they swallow each other up.
But separate again
for the joy of being two . . .
The entire universe
is too small to contain them.
Yet they live happily
in the tiniest particle.[1]

Such erotic affirmation of the world of phenomena is not limited to Hinduism. Ancient Goddess religions carry it too, as does Sufism in Islam and the Kabbalah in Judaism. Even Christianity has its tradition of bridal mysticism.

This view of world as lover also occurs outside of religious metaphor. A poet friend of mine, left by her partner, was catapulted into extreme grief and loneliness. Leaving her rural community, she moved to New York City, took a single bare room, and walked the city streets for months. Through walking, she eventually found her wholeness again. She said, "I learned to move in the world as if it were my lover."

In his little book *Cosmicomics*, Italian storyteller Italo Calvino describes the evolution of life from the perspective of an individual who experienced it from the beginning. Each chapter begins with a quote from science and one of them, which is titled "All in One Point," reads: "Through the calculations begun by Edwin P. Hubble on the galaxies' velocity of recession, we can establish the moment when all the universe's matter was concentrated in a single point, before it began to expand in space."

"We were all there, where else could we have been?" says Calvino's narrator, Qfwfq. He then goes on to describe his experience:

> We were all in that one point—and, man, was it crowded! Contrary to what you might think, it wasn't the sort of situation that encourages sociability. . . . Given the conditions, irritations were almost inevitable. See, in addition to all those people, you have to add all the stuff we had to keep piled up in there: all the material that was to serve afterwards to form the universe . . . from the nebula of Andromeda to the Vosges Mountains to beryllium isotopes. And on top of that we were always bumping against the Z'zu family's household goods: camp beds, mattresses, baskets. . . . [2]

So there were, naturally enough, complaints and gossip, but none ever attached to Signora Pavacini. (Since most names in the story have no vowels, I have given her a name we can pronounce.) "Signora Pavacini, her bosom, her thighs, her orange dressing gown," the sheer memory of her fills our narrator:

> with a blissful, generous emotion . . . the fact that she went to bed with her friend Mr. DeXueaux was well known. But in a point, if there's a bed, it takes up the whole point, so it isn't a question of *going* to bed but of *being* there, because anybody in the point is also in the bed. So consequently it was inevitable that she was in bed with each of us. If she'd been another person, there's no telling all the things that might have been said about her. . . . [3]

This state of affairs could have gone on indefinitely, but something extraordinary happened. An idea occurred to Signora Pavacini: "Oh boys, if only I had some room, how I'd like to make some pasta for you!" Here I quote, in part, from

my favorite longest sentence in literature, which closes this particular chapter in Calvino's collection:

> And in that moment we all thought of the space that her
> round arms would occupy moving backward and forward
> over the great mound of flour and eggs . . . while her arms
> kneaded and kneaded, white and shiny with oil up to the
> elbows, and we thought of the space the flour would occupy
> and the wheat for the flour and the fields to raise the wheat
> and the mountains from which the water would flow to irri-
> gate the fields . . . of the space it would take for the Sun to
> arrive with its rays, to ripen the wheat; of the space for the
> Sun to condense from the clouds of stellar gases and burn;
> of the quantities of stars and galaxies and galactic masses in
> flight through space which would be needed to hold sus-
> pended every galaxy, every nebula, every sun, every planet,
> and at the same time we thought of it, this space was inevita-
> bly being formed, at the same time that Signora Pavacini was
> uttering those words: " . . . ah, what pasta, boys!" the point
> that contained her and all of us was expanding in a halo of
> distance in light years and light centuries and billions of light
> millennia and we were being hurled to the four corners of
> the universe . . . and she dissolved into I don't know what
> kind of energy-light-heat, she, Signora Pavacini, she who in
> the midst of our closed, petty world had been capable of a
> generous impulse, "Boys, the pasta I could make for you!"
> a true outburst of general love, initiating at the same time
> the concept of space and, properly speaking, space itself, and
> time, and universal gravitation, and the gravitating universe,
> making possible billions and billions of suns, and planets,
> and fields of wheat, and Signoras Pavacinis scattered through
> the continents of the planets, kneading with floury, oil-shiny,
> generous arms, and she lost at that very moment, and we,
> mourning her loss.[4]

But is she lost? Or is she equally present, in every moment, her act of love embodied in every unfolding of this amazing world? Whether we see it as Krishna or as Signora Pavacini, that teasing, loving presence is in the monsoon clouds and the peacock's cry that heralds the monsoon, and in the plate of good pasta. For when you see the world as lover—if you have a clever, appreciative eye—every being can become an expression of that ongoing, erotic impulse. It takes form right now in each one of us and in everyone and everything we encounter—the bus driver, the neighbor on the corner, the leaping squirrel. As we seek to discover the lover in each life form, we can find ourselves in the dance of *rasa-lila*, sweet play, where each of the milkmaids who yearned for Krishna finds him magically at her side, her very own partner in the dance. The one beloved becomes many, and the world itself is her lover.

WORLD AS SELF

Just as lovers seek union, we are apt, when we fall in love with our world, to fall into oneness with it as well. We begin to see the world as belonging to us as intimately as our own bodies. Hunger for this union springs from a deep knowing, which mystics of all traditions give voice to. Breaking open a seed to reveal its life-giving kernel, the sage in the Upanishads tells his student: "*Tat tvam asi*—That art thou." In sum, the tree that will grow from the seed, that art thou; the running water, that art thou; and the sun in the sky, and all that is, that art thou.

"There is a Secret One inside us," says Kabir, "the planets in all the galaxies pass through his hands like beads." Mystics of the Abrahamic religions speak of merging self with God rather than with the world, but the import is often the same. When Hildegard of Bingen experienced unity with the divine, she gave it these words: "I am the breeze that nurtures all things green. . . . I am the rain coming from the dew that causes the grasses to laugh with the joy of life."

Indigenous traditions around the globe know the self as one with its world. Nature is alive and seamlessly whole, often symbolized by a circle: the sacred hoop of life. Not only our fate, but also our identity is interwoven with all beings. Native American writer-poet N. Scott Momaday sings it this way:

> I am a feather on the bright sky
> I am the blue horse that runs on the plain
> I am the fish that rolls, shining, in the water
> I am the shadow that follows a child . . .
> I am the hunger of a young wolf.
> I am the whole dream of these things
> You see, I am alive, I am alive[5]

The fifteenth-century cardinal Nicholas of Cusa defined God as an infinite circle whose periphery is nowhere and whose center is everywhere. That center, that one self, is in you and me and the tree outside the door. Similarly, the Jeweled Net of Indra, the vision of reality that arose with Hua Yen Buddhism, reveals a world where each being, each gem at each node of the net, is illumined by all the others and reflected in them. As part of this world, you contain the whole of it.

We don't have to surrender our individuality to experience the world as an extended self and its story as our own extended story. The liver, leg, and lung that are "mine" are highly distinct from each other, thank goodness, and each has a distinctive role to play. The larger "self" we discover is not an undifferentiated unity. As in all living systems, intelligence depends on the integrative play of diversity. Diversity is a source of resilience. This is good news, because this time of great challenge demands more commitment, endurance, and courage than any one of us can dredge up out of our own individual supply. We can learn to draw on the other neurons in the neural net and view them with gratitude. The acts and intentions of others are like seeds that can germinate and bear fruit through our own lives, as we take them in and dedicate that awareness to the healing of our world.

Now it can dawn on us: *we are the world knowing itself.* As we relinquish our isolation, we come home again to a world that can appear to us both as self and lover. Relating to our world with the full measure of our being, we partake of the qualities of both. In his poem "The Old Mendicant," Zen Master Thich Nhat Hanh evokes the long, wondrous evolutionary journey we all have made together, from which we are as inseparable as from our own selves. At the same time, it is a love song. Hear these lines, as if addressed to you:

> Being rock, being gas, being mist, being Mind,
> being the mesons traveling among galaxies at the speed
>   of light,
> you have come here, my beloved. . . .
> You have manifested yourself
> as trees, grass, butterflies, single-celled beings,
> and as chrysanthemums.
> But the eyes with which you looked at me this morning
> tell me you have never died.[6]

We have all gone on that long journey, and now, richer for it, we come home to our mutual belonging. We return to the experience that we are both the self of our world and its cherished lover. We are not doomed to destroy it by the cravings of the separate ego and the technologies it fashioned. We can wake up to who we really are, allow the rivers to flow clean once more, and the trees to grow green along their banks.

TWO

GROUNDING IN GRATITUDE

The root of joy is gratefulness . . .
It is not joy that makes us grateful;
it is gratitude that makes us joyful.

—BROTHER DAVID STEINDL-RAST

We have received an inestimable gift. To be alive in this beautiful, self-organizing universe—to participate in the dance of life with senses to perceive it, lungs that breathe it, organs that draw nourishment from it—is a wonder beyond words. And it is, moreover, an extraordinary privilege to be accorded a human life, with self-reflexive consciousness that brings awareness of our own actions and the ability to make choices. It lets us choose to join the praising and healing of our world.

Gratitude for the gift of life is a primary wellspring of all religions, hallmark of the mystic, fuel for the artist. Yet we so easily take this gift for granted. That is why so many spiritual traditions begin with thanksgiving, to remind us that for all our woes and worries, our existence itself is an unearned benefaction beyond any we could merit.

In the Tibetan Buddhist path, we are asked to pause before undertaking meditative practice and reflect on the preciousness of a human life. This is not because we as humans are superior to other beings, but because we can "change the karma." In other words, graced with self-reflexive consciousness, we are endowed with the capacity for choice—to take stock of what we are doing and change direction. We may have endured for eons of lifetimes as other life forms under the heavy hand of fate and the blind play of instinct, but now at last we are granted the ability to consider and judge and make decisions. Weaving our ever more complex neural circuits into the miracle of self-awareness, life yearned through us for the ability to know and act and speak on behalf of the larger whole. Now the time has come when we can consciously enter the dance.

In Buddhist practice, that first reflection is followed by a second, on the brevity of this precious human life: "Death is certain; the time of death is uncertain." That reflection awakens in us the marvelous gift of the present moment—to seize this chance to be alive right now on planet Earth.

EVEN IN THE DARK

That our world is in crisis—to the point where survival of conscious life on Earth is in question—in no way diminishes the value of this gift. On the contrary, to us is granted the privilege of being on hand to take part, if we choose, in the arising of a just and sustainable society. We can let life work through us, enlisting all our strength, wisdom, and courage, so that life itself can continue.

There is so much to be done, and time is so short. We can proceed, of course, out of grim and angry desperation. But the tasks progress more easily and productively with a measure of thankfulness for life; it links us to our deeper powers and lets us rest in them. Many of us are braced, psychically and physically, against the signals of distress that continually barrage us in the news, on our streets, and in the wider world. As if to reduce their impact on us, we withdraw like a turtle into its shell. But we can choose to turn to the breath, the body, the senses, for they help us to open to wider currents of knowing and feeling.

The great open secret of gratitude is that it is not dependent on external circumstance. It's like a setting or channel that we can switch to at any moment, no matter what's going on around us. It's a posture of the soul. Like the breath, it helps us affirm our basic right to be here.

Thankfulness loosens the grip of the consumer society by contradicting its hidden but pervasive message: that we are insufficient and inadequate. The forces of corporate capitalism continually tell us that we are needy—we need more stuff, more money, more approval, more comfort, more entertainment. The dissatisfaction it breeds is profound. It infects people with a compulsion to acquire that delivers them into the cruel bondage of debt. So gratitude is liberating. It builds a sense of sufficiency that is quite subversive to the consumer economy. Elders of indigenous cultures have retained this knowledge, and we can learn from them.

LEARNING FROM THE ONONDAGA

Elders of the six-nation confederacy of the Haudenosaunee, also known as the Iroquois, have passed down through the ages the teachings of the Great Peacemaker. A thousand years ago, these nations were warring tribes, caught in brutal cycles of attack, revenge, and retaliation, when the Great Peacemaker came across Lake Ontario in a stone canoe. Gradually his words and actions won them over and they accepted the Great Law of Peace. They buried their weapons under the Peace Tree by Lake Onondaga and formed councils for making wise choices together and for self-governance. In the Haudenosaunee, historians recognize the oldest known participatory democracy, and point to the inspiration it provided to Benjamin Franklin, James Madison, and others in crafting the Constitution of the United States. That did not, however, impede American settlers and soldiers from taking by force most of the Haudenosaunees' land and decimating their populations.

Eventually accorded "sovereign" status, the Haudenosaunee nations—all except for the Onondaga—proceeded in recent decades to sue state and federal governments for their ancestral lands, winning settlements in cash and license for casinos. All waited and wondered what legal action would be brought by the Onondaga Nation, whose name means Keepers of the Central Fire and whose ancestral land, vastly larger than the bit they now control, historically extended across a wide swath from Pennsylvania north into Canada. But the Onondaga elders and clan mothers continued to deliberate year after year, seeking consensus on this issue that would shape the fate of their people for generations to come. Finally, in the spring of 2005, they made their legal move. In their land rights claim, unlike that of any other indigenous claim at the time, they did not demand the return of any ancestral land or monetary compensation for it. They asked for one thing only: that it be cleaned up and restored to health for the sake of all who presently live on it and for the sake of their children and children's children.

To state and federal power-holders, this was asking a lot. The land is heavily contaminated by industrial development, including big chemical processing plants and a number of neglected toxic waste sites. Onondaga Lake, on whose shores stood the sacred Peace Tree, is considered to be more polluted with heavy metals than any other lake in the country. Within a year, at the urging of the governor of New York, the court dismissed the Onondaga claim as invalid and too late.

On a bleak November afternoon, when the lawsuit was still in process, I visited the Onondaga Nation—a big name for this scrap of land that looks like a postage stamp on maps of central New York State. I had come because I was moved by the integrity and vision of their land rights claim, and now I saw how few material resources they possessed to pursue it. In the community center, native counselors described outreach programs for mental health and self-esteem that bring young people together from all the Haudenosaunee. To help with the expenses, other tribes had chipped in, but few contributions had been received from the richer ones.

They were eager for me to see the recently built school where young Onondagans who choose not to go off the Nation to US-run schools can receive an education. One of the clan mothers, Freida, who was serving for a while as a teacher, had waited after hours to show me around. The central atrium she led me into was hung about with shields of a dozen clans—turtle clan, bear clan, frog—and on the floor, illumined by the skylight, was a large green turtle, beautifully wrought of inlaid wood. "Here is where we gather the students for our morning assembly," Freida explained. "We begin, of course, with the thanksgiving. Not the real, traditional form of it, because that takes days. We do it very short, just twenty minutes or so."

Turning to gaze at her face, I sank down on a bench. She heard my silent request and sat down too. Raising her right hand in a circling gesture that spiraled downward as the fingers closed, she began. "Let us gather our minds as one mind and give thanks to Grandfather Sun, who rises each day to bring light so we can see each other's faces and warmth for the seeds to grow." On and on she continued, greeting and thanking the life-giving presences that bless and nourish us all. With each one—moon, waters, trees—that lovely gesture was repeated. "We gather our minds as one mind."

My eyes stayed riveted on her. What I was receiving through her words and gesture felt like an intravenous injection, right into my bloodstream. This, I knew, could teach us how to survive when possessions and comforts have been lost. When our privileged place in the world is taken from us, this practice could hold us together in dignity and clarity of mind.

What Freida gave me is a staple of Haudenosaunee culture. Known as *"Ohenton Kariwahtekwen,"* which in English means "The Words That Come Before All Else," this is a bedrock tradition for most of indigenous North America. Soon after my visit with Freida, I looked for a written source open to everyone and found one online that Jake Swamp of the Mohawk Nation has offered.[1] In reading this, please note that the enumeration of the relatives follows a specific order as greetings and gratitude are offered to each. Native speakers usually speak their own words spontaneously, which always moves me. But as a Euro-American, I feel more comfortable sharing and using the words Jake Swamp chose to offer.

THE MOHAWK THANKSGIVING ADDRESS

The People

Today we have gathered and we see that the cycles of life continue. We have been given the duty to live in balance and harmony with each other and all living things. So now, we bring our minds together as one as we give greetings and thanks to each other as people.

Now our minds are One.

The Earth Mother

We are all thankful to our Mother, the Earth, for she gives us all that we need for life. She supports our feet as we walk about upon her. It gives us joy that she continues to care for us as she has from the beginning of time. To our Mother, we send greetings and thanks.

Now our minds are One.

The Waters

We give thanks to all the waters of the world for quenching our thirst and providing us with strength. Water is life. We know its power in many forms—waterfalls and rain, mists and streams, rivers and oceans. With One mind, we send greetings and thanks to the spirit of Water.

Now our minds are One.

The Fish

We turn our minds to all the Fish life in the water. They were instructed to cleanse and purify the water. They also give themselves to us as food. We are grateful that we can still find pure water. So, we turn now to the Fish and send our greetings and thanks.

Now our minds are One.

The Plants

Now we turn toward the vast fields of Plant life. As far as the eye can see, the Plants grow, working many wonders. They sustain many life forms. With our minds gathered together, we give thanks and look forward to seeing Plant life for many generations to come.

Now our minds are One.

The Food Plants

With One mind, we turn to honor and thank all the Food Plants we harvest from the garden. Since the beginning of time, the grains, vegetables, beans, and berries have helped the people survive. Many other living things draw strength from them too. We gather all the Plant Foods together as one and send them a greeting of thanks.

Now our minds are One.

The Medicine Herbs

Now we turn to all the Medicine herbs of the world. From the beginning they were instructed to take away sickness. They are always waiting and ready to heal us. We are happy there are still among us those special few who remember how to use these plants for healing. With One mind, we send greetings and thanks to the Medicines and to the keepers of the Medicines.

Now our minds are One.

The Animals

We gather our minds together to send greetings and thanks to all the Animal life in the world. They have many things to teach us as people. We are honored when they give up their lives so we may use their bodies as food for our people. We see them near our homes and in the deep forests. We are glad they are still here and we hope that it will always be so.

Now our minds are One.

The Trees

We now turn our thoughts to the Trees. The Earth has many families of Trees who have their own instructions and uses. Some provide us with shelter and shade, others with fruit, beauty, and other useful things. Many people of the world use a Tree as a symbol of peace and strength. With One mind, we greet and thank the Tree life.

Now our minds are One.

The Birds

We put our minds together as One and thank all the Birds who move and fly about over our heads. The Creator gave them beautiful songs. Each day they remind us to enjoy and appreciate life. The Eagle was chosen to be their leader. To all the Birds—from the smallest to the largest—we send our joyful greetings and thanks.

Now our minds are One.

The Four Winds

We are all thankful to the powers we know as the Four Winds. We hear their voices in the moving air as they refresh us and purify the air we breathe. They help us to bring the change of seasons. From the four directions they come, bringing us messages and giving us strength. With One mind, we send our greetings and thanks to the Four Winds.

Now our minds are One.

The Thunderers

Now we turn to the west where our Grandfathers, the Thunder Beings, live. With lightning and thundering voices, they bring with them the water that renews life. We are thankful that they keep those evil things made by Okwiseres underground. We bring our minds together as one to send greetings and thanks to our Grandfathers, the Thunderers.

Now our minds are One.

The Sun

We now send greetings and thanks to our eldest Brother, the Sun. Each day without fail he travels the sky from east to west, bringing the light of a new day. He is the source of all the fires of life. With One mind, we send greetings and thanks to our Brother, the Sun.

Now our minds are One.

Grandmother Moon

We put our minds together to give thanks to our oldest Grandmother, the Moon, who lights the nighttime sky. She is the leader of women all over the world, and she governs the movement of the ocean tides. By her changing face we measure time, and it is the Moon who watches over the arrival of children here on Earth. With One mind, we send greetings and thanks to our Grandmother, the Moon.

Now our minds are One.

The Stars

We give thanks to the Stars who are spread across the sky like jewelry. We see them in the night, helping the moon to light the darkness and bringing dew to the gardens and growing things. When we travel at night, they guide us home. With our minds gathered together as One, we send greetings and thanks to the Stars.

Now our minds are One.

The Enlightened Teachers

We gather our minds to greet and thank the enlightened Teachers who have come to help throughout the ages. When we forget how to live in harmony, they remind us of the way we were instructed to live as people. With One mind, we send greetings and thanks to these caring Teachers.

Now our minds are One.

The Creator

Now we turn our thoughts to the Creator, or Great Spirit, and send greetings and thanks for all the gifts of Creation. Everything we need to live a good life is here on this Mother Earth. For all the love that is still around us, we gather our minds together as One and send our choicest words of greetings and thanks to the Creator.

Now our minds are One.

Closing Words

We have now arrived at the place where we end our words. Of all the things we have named, it was not our intention to leave anything out. If something was forgotten, we leave it to each individual to send such greetings and thanks in their own way.

Now our minds are One.

GRATITUDE OPENS THE SPIRAL

There are hard things to face in our world today, if we want to be of use. Gratitude, when it's real, offers no blinders. In the face of devastation and tragedy it can ground us, especially when we're scared. It can hold us steady for the work to be done.

The activist's inner journey appears to me like a spiral, interconnecting four successive stages or movements that feed into each other. These four are (1) opening to gratitude, (2) honoring our pain for the world, (3) seeing with new eyes, and (4) going forth. The sequence repeats itself—ever in new ways—as the spiral circles round. The spiral is fractal in nature: it can characterize a lifetime or a project, it can unfold in a day or several times a day.

The spiral begins with gratitude, because that quiets the frantic mind and brings us back to source. It reconnects us with basic goodness, and it helps us be more fully present to our world. That grounded presence provides the psychic space for acknowledging the pain we carry for our world.

In honoring this pain, and daring to experience it, we learn the true meaning of *compassion*: to "suffer with." We begin to experience the immensity of our heart-mind and how it helps us to move through fear. What had isolated us in private anguish now opens outward and delivers us into wider contexts of belonging.

Our inter-existence with one another and with all beings is made real to us by our pain for the world and helps us see with new eyes. It brings into view webs of relationship through space and time. It shows us who we are and how we are related to each other and the universe. We begin to comprehend our own power to change and heal. We strengthen by growing living connections with past and future generations, and our cousin species.

Then, ever again, we go forth into action that calls us. With others, whenever and wherever possible, we set a target, lay a plan, step out. We don't wait for a blueprint or fail-proof scheme, for each step will be our teacher, bringing new perspectives and opportunities. Even when we don't succeed in a given venture, we can be grateful for the chance we took and the lessons we learned. And the spiral continues.

THREE

THE GATEWAY
OF DESPAIR

Let this darkness be a bell tower
and you the bell. As you ring,
what batters you becomes your strength.

—RAINER MARIA RILKE

The teaching of Akshobhya's mirror is fierce and unyielding: *Do not look away. Do not avert your gaze. Do not turn aside.* It was Jacques-Yves Cousteau who forced me to really look in the mirror. What I saw could not be denied. The experience itself is burned into my memory and led to my understanding that despair can be a gateway to awakening.

The year was 1977, and my son Jack was a freshman at Tufts University. When my daughter, Peggy, and I went to visit him for a weekend, he jubilantly told us he had scored tickets for the three of us to attend the Cousteau Society symposium on the environment at the Boston Coliseum. The symposium was a wealth of exhibits, panels, displays, and information on almost every environmental concern known at the time. We went from floor to floor, heard talk after talk, and I found the issues fascinating though familiar. As a family, we had joined an environmental study action group in Syracuse, and together with them learned a lot about a broad range of issues. If it weren't for what happened at the end of the day, I might have had a similar response to other meetings I'd attended: "Yes, it's pretty discouraging, but we'll pull through if we work on it."

In the late afternoon, Jack and Peggy took off for John Denver's concert, the symposium finale. I found myself slipping into an alcove to rest for a moment before heading back to Cambridge. Sitting there in the dark, I glanced at the video playing on repeat. Once it caught my eye, I could not stop looking. It was a scene on ice, a man with a cowboy hat, doing an intricate, methodical task on the ground between his booted feet. Looking closer, I saw he was clubbing a baby seal to death, pausing partway to relax and have a cigarette. I leaned in to peer at his face. I needed to see it because I knew it was *our* face. And this was just one small strand of what we were doing to the planet, one more thing we knew how to stop, yet we let political and economic forces block us every step of the way.

Heading home, the T came out of the subway tunnel and into the evening light, crossing a bridge over the Charles River. The view out the windows was idyllic, sailboats leaning into the wind at sunset, and at that moment, something gave way inside of me and tears streamed down my face. It felt as if all the information that for years had been stored up in my head, along with the scaffolding that held it in place, suddenly gave way, and the knowledge came cascading down through my whole body. Between the beauty of this world and the knowledge of what we are doing to it came a luminous and almost unbearable grief.

In the weeks that followed, I shared none of this with family and friends. I did not want them to be infected by my suffering, and I couldn't bear their trying to cheer me up or belittle my anguish. In our backyard at night, I would stay out late, gazing up at the starry sky, calling out in my heart to life on any other planets that might hear me. It would be some small consolation if our failure could be of use somewhere in this universe. When I did speak to a close colleague at the religion department, whose stock and trade was questions of meaning, his response was patronizing and dismissive. So, although daily life went on, I kept my despair in an inner chamber. It wasn't until fifteen months later, when I was invited to chair a week-long working group for the Society for Values in Higher Education at Notre Dame, that something finally broke open.

The name of the group that was to meet each morning was "The Human Prospect." To prepare for the sessions, I took along a book on the planet's current ecological conditions when I visited my son Chris on a wilderness farm in British Columbia. It was by Lester Brown, with the title *The Twenty-Ninth Day*. There I retreated for a few days to a cabin in the forest and read it at night by the fire. The title comes from a French children's riddle describing a lake where lily pads are growing, doubling their spread every day. The lake is totally covered on the thirtieth day. *On what day is the lake only half covered? The twenty-ninth day*. And I saw that now, in our lifetime, we were on the *twenty-ninth* day.

After reading this, and with what happened to me on the bridge over the Charles, I wondered whether I could bear to have the members of the working group start out by giving their academic title and rank and then reading their prepared papers. I wanted us to meet simply as humans on an endangered planet. I wanted to hear people's feelings about being alive now and know what they saw in Akshobhya's mirror. On the first morning, I asked everyone: "Please introduce yourself and share an experience where you've felt the planetary crisis impinge upon your own life." At the time, this was unusual, and as their words tumbled forth, so did our shared humanity.

As we completed the first day's session, the room teemed with energy. Participants kept on talking as they went off to lunch. Throughout the rest of the week, we found ourselves meeting often again throughout the day, making plans, sharing projects in the evenings, laughing together. We had broken through something, and it was like taking a lid off of a pot, this new kind of intimacy we felt with one another.

The last night of the conference we sat up late reflecting. We already knew the week would be unforgettable. But what had transpired? Was it grief work? No, we decided, because the losses we dared to face hadn't happened yet. It was more like despair work. People filtered off to their beds, but I sat at a table in the dormitory basement deep into the night. Next to a humming Coke machine, while Fran was asleep in our bed, I wrote for hours, the words pouring through me as I opened to what despair work might be. What I wrote that night would become essential to the calling that would shape my life for the next five decades.

THE SCOPE OF DESPAIR

As I write now, COVID-19 is taking its mammoth toll in worldwide statistics, cases, and deaths. Yet even aside from the pandemic, we continue to be bombarded by signals of distress—hurricanes, floods, massive job loss, economic decline, climate chaos, and as always, nuclear proliferation. Not surprisingly, we are feeling despair—a despair well merited by the machinery of mass death that we continue to create and serve. What is surprising is the extent to which we continue to hide this despair from ourselves and each other. As a society, we are caught between a sense of impending collapse and psychic paralysis in acknowledging it.

Whether or not we choose to accord them serious attention, we are barraged by data that render questionable the survival of our culture, our species, and even our planet as a viable home for complex life. These warnings, to those who do take them seriously, signal probabilities of collapse that are mind-boggling in scope. You do not need to see it all in order to recognize that it is the end of world as we know it. Just one angle or dimension—be it the oceans, the forests, or food production—if you care about it, is enough.

Despair, in this context, is not a macabre certainty of doom or a pathological condition of depression and futility. It is not a nihilism denying meaning or efficacy to human effort. Rather, as it is being experienced by increasing numbers of people across a broad spectrum of society, despair is the loss of the assumption that our species will inevitably pull through. It represents a genuine accession to the possibility that this planetary experiment will end, the curtain rung down, the show over.

To feel despair in such a cultural setting can bring with it a sense of isolation. The psychic dissonance can be so acute as to seem to border on madness. The distance between our inklings of apocalypse and the tenor of business as usual is so great that, though we may respect our own cognitive reading of the signs, we tend to imagine that it is *we*, not society, who are insane.

LINES OF DEFENSE

Turning toward our despair is not as simple as it might sound. There are many ways we modern people impede our experience of despair and protect ourselves from truly knowing what we know. We can stop ourselves from feeling through psychic numbing. Then, once we feel it, we often hide it, and in addition, we may treat despair as an illness or personal pathology.

Psychic numbing. When we are fearful and the odds are running against us, it is easy to let the heart and mind go numb. Because the perils facing us are so pervasive, this numbing touches us all. No one is unaffected by it. No one is immune to doubt, denial, or disbelief about the severity of our situation. Yet of all the dangers we face, from climate chaos to nuclear warfare, none is so great as the deadening of our response.

Activists and their organizations, trying to arouse us to the fact that our survival is at stake, decry public apathy. The cause of our apathy, however, is not indifference. It stems from a fear of the despair that lurks beneath the tenor of daily life. A dread of what is happening to our future stays on the fringes of awareness, too deep to name and too fearsome to face. Because of social taboos against despair and because of the fear of pain, these can be hard to acknowledge or express directly. They are kept at bay.

The refusal to feel takes a heavy toll. It not only impoverishes our emotional and sensory life—flowers are dimmer and less fragrant, our loves less ecstatic—but psychic numbing also impedes our capacity to process and respond to information. The energy expended in resisting despair is diverted from more creative uses, depleting the resilience and imagination needed for fresh visions and strategies. Fear of despair erects an invisible screen, filtering out anxiety-provoking data. In a world where organisms require feedback in order to adapt and survive, this is suicidal.

Concealing. In India, at a leprosarium, I once met a young mother of four. Her leprosy was advanced, the doctor pointed out, because for so long she had hidden its signs. Fearing ostracism and banishment, she had covered her sores with her sari, pulled the shoulder drape around so no one would see. In a similar fashion did I later hide my despair for our world, cloaking it like a shameful disease—and so, I have learned, do others.

Despair is tenaciously resisted because it represents a loss of control, an admission of powerlessness. The acknowledgment of despair for the future is a kind of social taboo, especially here in America, and those who break it are considered depressed and depressing, unable to control their feelings. No one wants a Cassandra around or welcomes a Banquo to the feast. Nor are such roles enjoyable to play. When the prospect of our collective suicide first hit me as a serious possibility, I felt that there was no one I could turn to in my grief. I have loving, intelligent friends and family—but what could I say? Do I want them to feel this fear and horror too? What can be said without casting a pall or without seeming to ask for unacceptable words of comfort and cheer?

Pathologizing. To ease our suffering, we persuade ourselves that we need treatment and pills. Some of us even persuade ourselves that we are mentally ill and in need of care. The highly profitable pharmaceutical industry is more than ready to cater to such needs.

Psychotherapy, by and large, has offered limited help for coping with these feelings and, more often, tends to patholo-gize them. Many therapists have difficulty crediting the notion that concerns for the general welfare of our planet might be acute enough to cause distress. Trained to assume that all our drives are ego-centered, they tend to treat expressions of this distress as manifestations of personal neurosis. I often hear from students and readers the kinds of response they receive when, in a psychotherapeutic hour, they express their grief or anger over an ecological or social issue: "What might this concern represent that you are avoiding in your own life?" In such a way is our anguish for our world delegitimized. In my own case, deep dismay over destruction of a nearby forest was diagnosed by a psychotherapist as fear of my own libido or sexual drive (which the bulldozers were said to symbolize), and my painful preoccupation with US bombings of Vietnam was interpreted as an unwholesome hangover of Puritan guilt. Such "therapy," of course, only intensifies the sense of isolation and craziness that despair can bring.

At the root of our difficulty in accepting the genuine depth of human concern and even pain for the world lies a dysfunctional notion of the self. It is the notion of the self as an isolated and fragile entity. So long as we see ourselves as essentially separate, competitive, and ego-identified beings, it is difficult to respect the validity of our social despair. Both our capacity to grieve for others and our power to cope with this grief spring from the great matrix of relationships from which we arise. We are, as open systems, sustained by flows of energy and information that extend beyond the reach of the conscious ego.

RESPECTING DESPAIR

Let us, first of all, disabuse ourselves of the notion that grief for our world is morbid. To experience anguish and anxiety in the face of the perils that threaten us is a healthy reaction. Far from being crazy, this pain is a testimony to the unity of life, the deep interconnections that relate us to all beings. Pain for the world is not only natural, it is a necessary component of our ability to respond. As in all organisms, pain has a purpose: it is a warning signal, designed to trigger remedial action. It is not to be banished by injections of optimism or sermons on "positive thinking." It is a healthy, normal human response to the situation we find ourselves in. Faced and experienced, its power can be used. As the frozen defenses of the psyche thaw, new energies and intelligence are released to help us face the loss of meaning we are confronting.

Despair work is different from grief work in that its aim is not acceptance of loss—indeed, the losses we are witnessing are hardly to be viewed as acceptable. But it is similar in the dynamics unleashed by the willingness to acknowledge, feel, and express inner pain. From my own work and that of others, I know that we can come to terms with apocalyptic anxieties in ways that are integrative and liberating, opening awareness not only to planetary distress but also to the hope inherent in our own capacity to change.

POSITIVE DISINTEGRATION

In facing Akshobhya's mirror, our grief and fear and rage may make it seem as if we ourselves are coming unraveled, like our world. It can help to realize that falling apart is not such a bad thing. Indeed, it is as essential to evolutionary and psychological transformations as the cracking of outgrown shells. Polish psychiatrist Kazimierz Dabrowski calls it "positive disintegration." He sees it in every global development of humanity, especially during periods of accelerated change, where it functions to permit the emergence of more complex psychic structures and wider awareness. On the individual level, positive disintegration occurs when a person courageously confronts anomalies and contradictions of experience. It can bring on a dark night of the soul, a time of spiritual void and turbulence, but the anxieties and doubts are, Dabrowski maintains, "essentially healthy and creative."[1] They are creative not only for the person but also for society, because they permit new and timely approaches to reality.

What "disintegrates" in periods of rapid transformation is not the self, but its defenses and ideas. We are not objects that can break. As open systems, we are, in the words of Norbert Wiener, "but whirlpools in a river of everflowing water. We are not stuff that abides, but patterns that perpetuate themselves."[2] We do not need to protect ourselves from change, for our very nature is change. Defensive self-protection restricts vision and movement like a suit of armor and makes it far harder to adapt. It not only reduces flexibility but also blocks the flow of information we need to survive. Our "going to pieces," however uncomfortable, can facilitate new perceptions, new data, and new responses.

OPENING TO THE SUFFERING OF OTHERS

Our religious traditions can also serve to validate despair and attest to its life-giving function. The Biblical concept of the suffering servant, as well as an array of Old Testament prophets, speaks to the power inherent in opening ourselves to the suffering of others. In Christianity, the paramount symbol of such power is the cross. To my understanding and experience, the cross on which Jesus died serves to dramatize that it is precisely through openness to the pain of our world that redemption and renewal are found.

The heroes of the Mahayana Buddhist tradition are the bodhisattvas, who vow to forswear nirvana until all beings are enlightened. As the Lotus Sutra tells us, their compassion endows them with supranormal senses: they can hear the music of the spheres and understand the language of the birds. By the same token, they hear as well all cries of distress, even the moaning of beings in the lowest layers of hell. All griefs are registered and owned in the bodhisattva's deep knowledge that we are not separate from each other.

The Vietnamese poet and Zen teacher Thich Nhat Hanh was once asked, "What do we most need to do to save our world?" His questioners expected him to either emphasize the power of meditation or identify strategies for social and environmental action. But Thich Nhat Hanh simply said, "What we most need to do is to hear within us the sound of the Earth crying."[3]

That is what my colleagues and I began to do at the end of the 1970s—find ways we can break through the trance and help each other hear Earth crying within us. Drawing from systems theory and Buddhist teachings, we work mainly in groups, because the situation we face bears on us all. In sharing our innermost responses to the perils of our time, we rediscover our mutual belonging in the web of life and the capacity that it brings to act on life's behalf.

Despair and Empowerment work was the name first attached to our discovery and the theory and practice to which it led us. Over the years, other names followed, such as Deep Ecology work and the Work That Reconnects. Although the group work soon included other stages and features, the owning and honoring of our pain for the world has remained essential. Rainforest activist John Seed, a facilitator of this work, explains it this way: "You discover that others aren't afraid of your pain for the world, and you witness theirs. Then you can dare to hope something for humanity and for what we can do together. When we unblock our despair, everything else follows—the respect and awe, the love."[4]

TRUTH TELLING

When our feelings and experience of the world are finally expressed, it is like awakening from a trance. As Rev. angel Kyodo williams says, "We don't have to know the answers. We just have to choose to live into the truth."[5] Despair work involves nothing more mysterious than an honest sharing of what we see and know and feel is happening to our world. This is not so easy. Not only are there well-established lines of defense, but in our current culture, people have come to feel dependent on experts and are therefore timid and unsure when speaking about world conditions. This hesitation serves those in power, tending to create a climate of fear and obedience. Yet when we break that silence, it is liberating, and we find that the truth feels suddenly necessary, like oxygen. When we help each other to tell the truth and open to the feelings that go with it, we validate our common experience, forge bonds of solidarity, and develop an appetite for honesty.

A formal practice of intentional truth sharing has been modeled worldwide, inspired by the first Truth and Reconciliation Commission in South Africa. Since then, truth commissions have been established in many other countries, including Australia, Argentina, Canada, and Chile. To attest publicly to one's own role in a tragedy—and to the trauma one has suffered—requires courage and generates strength in return. These commissions have a powerful role to play in our time, teaching us ways to mend what has been broken and restore the integrity of victims and perpetrators alike.

In Colombia, after more than five decades of violence and conflict between paramilitaries, the army, and guerrilla forces, as well as the forced displacement of six million people, a truth commission was established in 2018. To bring the wounded and bitterly divided ethnic and political groups into conversation, the commission adopted the trained approach and methods of the Work That Reconnects. Now, in the wake of fifty years of enmity, betrayal, and slaughter, common ground is being found at last. It is found in the arms of grief, where the longing for healing arises and trust begins, anchored now in the all-embracing *Madre Tierra*.

Truth telling, of course, is an essential part of effective social and environmental activism, beaming a spotlight on what needs to change and why. Often, however, necessary information about the issue at stake is drowned out by the blistering charge of anger over the existing problem. How do we handle both feelings and facts? I have seen how prior sessions of despair work can yield a calm, disciplined concentration that is very effective in highly charged action.

I think of the nightly protests in forty cities after George Floyd's public suffocation by Minneapolis police. The rage was so deep and the cause so obvious, no expression of emotion could be sufficient. The outrage could only be dramatically matched by the sustained nonviolence of crowds of predominantly Black youth, supported by young people and older people of various races and backgrounds. This brought the reality of systemic injustice and racism into the consciousness of our nation as never before. As those in the movement called out the truths of injustice, they claimed the authority of their own voices.

Despair work is not a solo venture. It is a process undertaken within the context of community. When we face the darkness and terror of our time, openly and together, we tap deep reserves of strength. The gateway of despair opens to belonging. We think despair condemns us to isolation because it seems so taboo in our culture. But as we find again and again, what despair reveals is the depth of our caring. We hurt because we care. We are liberated when we realize that at the heart of our despair is our love for the world, our love of life itself.

FOUR

WISDOM
AND ACTION

Our own pulse beats in every stranger's throat.

—BARBARA DEMING

The notion that ethical action is something added on to one's concept of reality or the self is mistaken. In the Dharma, there are no "oughts" and no "shoulds." They disappear in the realization of *paticca samuppada*, the interdependent co-arising of all things. Instead of commandments from on high, there is the simple, profound awareness that *everything* is interwoven and mutually conditioning—each thought, word, and act, and all beings, too, are intertwined in the dance of reciprocity. Once insight is gained into this core teaching of the Buddha, certain ways of living and behaving emerge as intrinsic to it. Wisdom and moral action, *prajña* and *sila*, are then seen as inseparable as "two hands washing each other," to quote an early sutra. It is not one, then the other—they are simultaneous and complementary.

We can think of sila as our moral compass, an orientation that arises with insight. This compass helps us find our bearings in a world of hunger and conflict. As we come to see with new eyes, we can turn to this compass for direction. From the very outset there is a deep moral thrust to the Dharma, rooted in the radical relativity of all phenomena.

The Buddha's teaching of *anatta*, no-self, is one way of expressing paticca samuppada, and it reveals that the "I," the ego, the sense that we exist as separate entities, is actually a fiction. It is a convention, a useful one to be sure, but one to which we need not be in service. Because there is no self that needs to be defended, enhanced, or improved, the realization of that truth releases us into action that is free from the burdens of selfhood. Not confined by the prison cell of ego, we are liberated into those wider dimensions of life that are our true home.

Such action is not a burden that we nobly assume, as in "I am going out to save the world." That is the context for burning out. But when you experience taking action as an expression of your true nature, then your concept of reality and your response to it are inseparable. Seeing with new eyes, you go forth. Each act then becomes a way of affirming and knowing afresh the reality that the teaching expresses.

That also affects our ideas of what non-attachment is and what power is. Some gurus preach a non-attachment that appears suspiciously akin to sublime indifference, as if one should or could remain unmoved by the sufferings of others. With interdependent co-arising, this is impossible, for we see ourselves as participating in the existence of all beings and in the world we cocreate with them. Dharma non-attachment is from ego, not from the world.

POWER IN RECIPROCITY

In a hierarchical model of reality, such as found in theistic or god-centered religious traditions, the ascent to Divinity or pure

Mind tends to involve rising above the material world, equating what is real with what does not change. Whether it is conceived of as an immutable God or as a Brahman above space and time, it is essentially and ontologically distinct from the apparent messiness and randomness of nature. In this view, there is the temptation to escape from the disorderliness and suffering of "this" world to that changeless realm of pure order.

The staggeringly bold move of the Buddha was to see that the real is what *inheres* in change rather than being removed from change. That is the meaning of Dharma: the dynamics or "law" by which things change, the way things work. And that law—which the Buddha called Dharma and, more specifically, paticca samuppada—that law is such that every act we make, every word we speak, every thought we think is not only affected by other elements but also produces effects so far-reaching we cannot fully see or imagine them. We proceed with the act for its own worth, our sense of responsibility arising from our participation in all life.

As the Buddha revealed, there is order, but it is not based on a timeless, changeless being. It had been assumed, and often still is, that if there is order, there must be that which creates it; there must be mind over and against nature, so to speak. But in the view of paticca samuppada, life itself is its own dynamic order. The same goes for how we construe power. In a hierarchical construction of reality, everything is understood in terms of one-way linear causality. We've been conditioned by that view since Aristotle, and it has dominated both religion and science for over two millennia. Consequently, power is seen as directed from the top down. It is essentially power-*over* and is equated with domination, having one's way, pushing things

around, being as invulnerable to change as possible. Such a
view of power requires defenses, whether of the ego or clan or
nation-state.

With interdependent co-arising, causality is not linear and
unidirectional; it is nonlinear and reciprocal. Here power is a
two-way street. It is not power-over, but power-*with*, where
beings mutually affect each other. The old linear idea is essentially a zero-sum game: "you win, I lose." But this is breaking down now as more and more people are talking about and
wanting to play a "win-win game." That idea is very close to the
systems notion of synergy, which literally means "power-with"
and which requires no defenses because it operates through
openness. This is the kind of power we find at play in an ecosystem or neural net, where open reciprocal interaction is essential
to skillful functioning, as well as emergence of intelligence and
beauty. It is also the power of the bodhisattva, of the "boundless
heart" that opens to the griefs and joys of all beings.

THE WELFARE OF ALL BEINGS

One of the great heroes of Buddhist tradition is King Ashoka,
who, in his devotion to the Dharma, built hospitals and public
wells and tree-lined roads for the welfare of all beings. Historians recognize his efforts back then, in the third century BCE, as
the first social service program in recorded history.

Shantideva, the beloved and highly influential saint of the
eighth century, saw service as the path leading to enlightenment. On this path, you learn to put others' needs above your
own, even at the risk of your own well-being. Such generosity
fosters the transcendence of self, and it may lead you to the

experience more directly than sitting on your meditation cushion for years and years. In my own teaching, I have found that people are deeply moved by role-play exercises in which they speak from the perspective of another being, an adversary, or another species. By "exchanging self for other," as Shantideva put it, they find the shift they make takes them beyond ego's domain and engages their empathy and creativity.

After graduate school, in 1979, I saw for myself how these principles were put into action in community development when I devoted a year to "participant research" with the Buddhist-inspired Sarvodaya movement in Sri Lanka. From reading early scriptures, I had been thinking that the Buddha's Dharma could, in the future, be helpful to us all collectively, and as I shared that thought with a leader of an Indian ashram, he told me to go see what was happening with Sarvodaya. What I learned there changed my life. Right in front of me, I could see the contagious interplay of wisdom and action, as natural as two hands washing each other.

The Sarvodaya movement as a whole and in its village programs was clearly based on social ethics principles and practices, derived directly from early Buddhism, combined with a strong ethos from Vinoba Bhave and Gandhi. In 1983, a bloody and deeply polarizing civil war began and radically changed the whole country, making chasms out of ethnic, religious, and linguistic differences. Traumatizing brutalities on all sides have taken a tragic toll from which Sri Lanka has yet to recover. The assumptions and culture upon which the movement operated were greatly weakened. What moved me most deeply then can no longer be assumed to characterize Sarvodaya today. But I am still inspired by the values and strategies that I came to know

from personal experience. Having seen how effective and functional they were for the quarter century before the civil war, I
believe they have relevance for all of us today.

Of all the aspects and strategies of Sarvodaya, what caught
my attention and even enthusiasm the most was the practice of
shramadana. After a couple of months with the movement, I
chose to give it my full attention. On many a weekend I headed
out on my motorcycle to a village to participate with relish and
watch how the familiar drama unfolded in a different setting
with each new project.

The word *shramadana* means the "giving (*dana*) of
human energy (*shrama*)." The movement's full name, Sarvodaya Shramadana Sangamaya, literally means "the movement
of everybody waking up by working together." Generosity, or
dana, is a preeminent Buddhist virtue; in no other tradition is
it accorded so central a position. I loved seeing how dana was
reframed from being only almsgiving for the monks to include
labor, gifts of food, and sharing of entertainment. What Sarvodaya did was to liberate dana and present it as the sharing of
one's time, energy, skills, knowledge, and food with the community. So people would "wake up" by giving.

During my fieldwork in Sri Lanka in the 1980s, I was convinced that a chief strength of the movement was that it asked
people what they could *give* rather than what they wanted to
get, and it then provided opportunities to offer that in the shramadana camps. A village would ask for a shramadana camp and
a Sarvodaya organizer would work with them to plan and prepare their event, sharing Sarvodaya principles through action
rather than explanation. These camps hosted collective work
projects such as cutting access roads, digging latrines, roofing

the school. Even the poorest families were expected to contribute not only their labor but also food for the collective meal and songs and ideas in the meetings. I learned how empowering this was for everybody to be expected to give something. Even if you could give only a betel leaf or matchbox of rice, you would walk differently on the earth as a gift bestower.

The spirit of Sarvodaya has continued to influence other Buddhist movements in South and Southeast Asia. The vision and practices of shramadana have served as a model for elements in my own workshops and intensives, grounding wisdom and action in collaborative life experience. This has been true even among Asian Buddhists and leaders as eminent as the Dalai Lama, who, in reading my book on Sarvodaya, was quite taken with the descriptions of shramadana camps as possible models for his monks.

For some time, I've been part of the work of the International Network of Engaged Buddhists (INEB), which was first developed by my friend and global movement leader Sulak Sivaraksa, well-known as a dissident of Thailand. This stirring network expanded to reach socially engaged Buddhists around the world and is now helping communities work together collaboratively to meet the coronavirus pandemic. INEB's website showcases numerous examples applying Buddhist principles to social challenges. Their core mission is "to confront and end suffering using analysis and action guided by the Four Noble Truths." At the heart of their work is the value of *kalyanamitra*, or "spiritual friendship."

As the world came to grips with the COVID-19 pandemic, INEB called out the need to confront racial discrimination and stereotyping on the rise in reaction to uncertainty and economic instability. They are highlighting strategies to support equality, cultural diversity, and coexistence as critical to our times. In what they are calling a Buddhist Practice for Social Harmony, they draw on the Four Noble Truths as a guide to action. The First Noble Truth is represented by "creating a safe space for the oppressed to speak and offering deep listening to the suffering of others." The Second Noble Truth calls out structural and cultural causes of oppression. The Third Noble Truth, that there is a path to awakening, is expressed by "promoting feelings of mutual accommodations and gratitude among communities." And the action steps of the Fourth Noble Truth are "collaborative activities to support each other's communities"—in other words, to be spiritual friends together.

Since 2012, INEB has participated in the Inter-Religious Climate and Ecology Network. This interfaith network has worked to influence climate policy in Asia and to raise awareness among faith leaders and faith communities around the climate crisis. They support community actions for mitigation and adaptation that are "rooted in long-term sustainability and equitable development." Building spiritual friendships across political boundaries, they help hold the space for conversations between cultures on climate health and collaborative action.

THE FOUR ABODES

When I was living with the Sarvodaya movement, I found they took very seriously the Buddhist teaching of the four Brahmaviharas, also known as the Four Immeasurables, which my friends referred to as the Four Abodes of the Buddha. The Four Abodes were translated into day-to-day behavior not just by clergy but also by laypeople and children. These abodes—*metta* (lovingkindness), *karuna* (compassion), *mudita* (joy in the joy of others), and *upekkha* (equanimity)—were on the lips of every village organizer and painted on the walls of Sarvodaya village centers.

In the sutra in which this teaching appears, the Buddha was approached by Brahma priests who asked him, "How do you, respected teacher, bring someone to Brahma's abode?" In their own tradition, entry was only possible through an expensive, complex, and secret ceremony under the sole control of the priests. They expected that the Buddha would discredit himself publicly by saying that he didn't believe in the god Brahma or even, for that matter, in rituals. The Buddha surprised them by responding that he helps people experience heaven, or Brahma's abode, *right away*—through metta, karuna, mudita, and upekkha.

Although a primary dictum of the Judeo-Christian ethical tradition is to love your neighbor as yourself, we are not told *how* to do it. It is not always easy to love people. It might be easy to love people in general, but how to you love somebody you don't even like? The Buddhist tradition, with its high regard for skillful means, offers many ways to do this. These teachings can be lubricants and motivators giving momentum to skillful personal and social change. Qualities such as love and compassion are not just abstract virtues of saints and adepts; anyone should be able to experience these qualities in themselves. As the Buddha said, *ehi passiko*, "come and see." You don't even have to be a Buddhist; come and see for yourself with your own experience.

There is a meditation practice for developing the quality of metta (lovingkindness), the first abode. This involves holding someone in your mind and experiencing your desire that this person be free from fear, from greed, free from sorrow and the causes of suffering. The traditional meditation begins by focusing on one's self with these wishes and then addressing family members and friends, then one's enemies, and finally all beings. Taking time to internally identify with your desire that another be free from suffering can change the whole ambiance of a conflicting relationship. It builds endurance, and it releases our tremendous capacity for love. (Guided meditations that highlight the Four Abodes can be found in the back of the book.)

The second abode, karuna (compassion), is the practice of identifying with the suffering of others, learning to experience their pain as your own. We are often reluctant to experience pain, because we think we'll fall apart, or we don't want to look at a problem unless we know the solution. Buddhism teaches that the first step is simply to experience the pain. We won't fall apart because, as interconnected open systems, we can't fall apart. The ability to respond creatively and skillfully will arise naturally out of this openness.

The third abode, mudita (joy in the joy of others), is a quality we tend to overlook. It is the flip side of compassion, and to the extent that you can experience the suffering of another as your own, you can also learn to experience the joy of another as your own. The synergy that is inherent in interdependent co-arising is made available through taking joy in the joy of others. The courage of Martin Luther King or the endurance of Sojourner Truth does not stop with them but is ours as well, by virtue of our own inter-existence with all. We can draw on this imaginatively by seeing that the good done by any being, past or present, enters into this reality structure in which we exist and is a resource for us to strengthen our own intentions. Anyone with whom we come in contact—family, friends, the person next to you at the checkout counter—all have goodness and capacities that we can open to and share in. Looking at things this way helps release us from envy and competitiveness, which are such energy drains.

The fourth abode, upekkha, is usually translated as "equanimity" or "impartiality," but those terms can seem less compelling. As with the others, upekkha springs from paticca samuppada, the co-arising web in which we take being. As we regard another, we can let our consciousness sink within like a stone, below the level of word and deed to the depths of our co-arising. In each moment, it arises in new forms, but underneath the dynamic unfolding of reality persists and sustains, and in that web we can rest. Out of it we cannot fall. Below the separate "I's" that arise over time, that net is what we are, and in it we find the great peace of upekkha.

The awareness of interbeing that we discover through this pain for all beings is the ever-deepening appreciation of paticca samuppada. Co-arising and inseparable, we can never fall out of the web of belonging. Opening to its presence and resilience, we can trust. Moving beyond ego fears, we can risk, we can take action for the sake of all beings. This is where we find our ultimate bearings and our source of action. Act, as the Buddha said, *bahujana hitaya bahujana sukhaya,* "for the sake of all beings and for their happiness."

PART TWO

Food for the Mind

FIVE

THE WHEEL
OF INTERBEING

This being, that becomes;
from the arising of this, that arises;
this not being, that becomes not;
from the ceasing of this, that ceases.

—MAJJHIMA NIKAYA, II, 32

The eight-spoked wheel that graces gateways and temple roofs throughout the Buddhist world symbolizes the teaching of the Buddha. It is called the Wheel of the Dharma, the *Dharma Chakra*. It also represents the central doctrine that his teachings convey: the doctrine of paticca samuppada, the interdependent co-arising of all phenomena. This centerpiece of the Buddha's teaching is not about a dimension of reality separate from our daily lives. It refers not to an absolute or eternal essence, but to the way things work, how events happen and relate to each other. Perceiving all existence as a dynamic, self-sustaining web of relations, it stood in stark contrast to the other schools of thought in the Buddha's time.

I was drawn to Buddhism long before I grasped the importance of this doctrine. It took me nine years before I realized how remarkable and distinctive this teaching is and how it casts a clarifying light on every other aspect of Buddhist thought and practice. What had drawn me to the Dharma was the luminous vitality of Buddhists I knew in Asia and the meditative practices they showed me. All the while, the scriptural discourses on causality struck me as musty and remote. This doctrine seemed either so obvious (everything has a cause, often multiple causes) or so abstruse (with scholastic enumerations of causal factors) as to appear irrelevant to my own life. I figured I could bracket that aspect of Buddhist philosophy and devote my studies to more engaging topics such as the compassionate way of the bodhisattva.

I believed that insights and practices offered in Buddhism could be liberating to Westerners, so after my return from Asia I enrolled in a graduate program at Syracuse University to study Buddhism more formally and obtain credentials to teach in American institutions. I began to study deeply the early scriptures with a particular focus: *What is so distinctive in the Buddha's teachings? Why do their moral values and spiritual practices seem so compelling?* Other religions upheld similar ideals of compassion and nonviolence, generosity and self-restraint; other faiths acknowledged the same kinds of responsibility and service. But in the Buddhadharma these ethical norms had a transparent, unburdened quality. Why, in the Buddhist context, did they feel so accessible, so liberating? I sensed that there was something extremely important that was eluding me, but I was unable to bring it into focus.

Related questions arose: According to most Western religious thought, ethical values derive from divine commandment. Without the ontological security of belief in an unchanging absolute, everything seems awash, with no clear guidelines, and it's "every man for himself." This assumption is so pervasive that even noted Western scholars judged Buddhism's moral teachings to be weak, since they do not issue from belief in any supernatural authority. Indeed, when he was asked by what authority he spoke, the Buddha cited again and again: paticca samuppada, the law of interdependent co-arising—not any entity *ruling* our world, but the dynamics at work *within* our world. What did he mean by that? How can radical relativity serve as moral grounding?

With fascination I studied the early Buddhist texts. I read how paticca samuppada dawned on the Buddha the night of his enlightenment and was always described as the conceptual content of that awakening. I saw how it underlay everything he taught about the self and its suffering and its liberation from suffering. I noted how it knocked down the dichotomies bred by hierarchical thinking, the old polarities between mind and matter, self and world, that had exasperated me as a spiritual seeker, as an activist, and as a woman. I saw how it brought the Buddha into conflict with the religious beliefs of his day, distancing him from earlier philosophic thought. I saw it as consonant with the systems thinking emerging in our own time, and I saw how it could help us understand the implications of this new process paradigm. Indeed, I felt as if I had come upon a whole fresh way of looking at things.

INTERDEPENDENT CO-ARISING

Siddhartha Gautama, the man who became the Buddha, left a life of luxury and privilege to seek liberating wisdom. Under highly reputed masters, he engaged in years of advanced yogic practices and then, after that, extreme austerities. But he found nothing that could explain or resolve the dilemma at the core of human experience: how we create suffering for ourselves and for others. He finally stopped wandering, and relying on his own unswerving determination, he sat in the shade of a fig tree, vowing to stay there until he gained insight into this mystery.

With his back to the tree, he began not with abstractions or religious beliefs, but with his own experience. To anchor his attention, he steadied himself with the elemental process of breathing in and breathing out. With that simple practice, he was free to trace how the basic factors of being alive, such as awareness, sensation, feeling, and wanting, give rise to each other. In so doing, he found no linear first cause or prime mover. Instead he beheld patterns and circuits of contingency—arising, ceasing, and sustaining by virtue of their interplay. It was then, in the crucible of his unwavering attention, that the realization of interdependent co-arising swept upon him.

The Mahapadana Sutta says:

> Coming to be, coming to be! . . . Ceasing to be, ceasing to be! At that thought, brethren, there arose . . . a vision of things not before called to mind, and knowledge arose. . . . Such is form, such is the coming to be of form, such is its passing away. Such is cognition, such is its coming to be, such is its passing away. And [he abided] in the discernment of the arising and passing away.[1]

The process nature of reality became clear. He beheld the flowing interaction of all things, as they provide occasion and context for each other's emergence and subsiding—each as real as the air we breathe, each as transient as a thought. All aspects of our world and all factors of our lives subsist, he saw, in a dynamic web of interdependence. To the physical eye, we look like separate projects walking around in separate bodies. And, as such, we vie with each other for a place in the sun and compete for resources to meet our own private needs and desires. Still, the fact of our interdependence suggests that we are capable of seeing and interacting in more harmonious ways, like living parts of a single living whole. Arising out of the web of life, our mutual belonging is not a vain and sentimental dream.

One of the earliest formulations of the central teaching was a four-part statement:

This being, that becomes;
from the arising of this, that arises;
this not being, that becomes not;
from the ceasing of this, that ceases.[2]

According to this apparently simple set of assertions, things do not produce each other or make each other happen, as in linear causality. They *help* each other happen by providing occasion or locus or context, and in so doing, they in turn are affected. There is a reciprocal dynamic at play. Power inheres not in any one dominating entity, but in the relationship between entities.

To address the issue of human suffering, the Buddha was called to teach and share his insights. Immersed in paticca samuppada, he gave rise to his first powerful teaching, the Four Noble Truths. In their traditional and highly condensed form, these are the truth of suffering (*dukkha*), the truth about the cause of our suffering (*samudaya*), the truth of the cessation of suffering (*nirodha*), and the path (*magga*) leading to its cessation. As they are elaborated throughout the Buddha's teachings, their meanings become richly relevant to our lives.

The First Noble Truth invites us to acknowledge the suffering we cause ourselves and each other and the frustrations endemic to our lives. With the Second Noble Truth, we recognize that we create our own bondage, as we try to grasp and identify with what is essentially impermanent. The Third Noble Truth would have us realize that suffering, arising in this fashion, is not inevitable; it can cease as we learn to recognize the interplay of all things. With the Fourth Noble Truth, we determine to walk the path that embodies this learning and cleanse our perceptions through meditation and ethical conduct.

After exploring this teaching in the early Buddhist scriptures, I discovered that its basic assumptions converged with those of general systems theory and the self-organizing nature of open systems. That encounter preoccupied two years of my life, as I compared and wove together the Buddhist and systems views of causality. I also found it in Sri Lanka, where I went to study the Buddhist-inspired community development movement called Sarvodaya Shramadana. There, paticca samuppada was the foundational operating principle that generated the goals and methods in which organizers were trained and villagers enlisted to work together. Most recently, I encountered paticca samuppada in the field of ecology, especially in what is called "deep ecology," a way of thinking and seeing that takes the logical step of moving beyond anthropocentrism in recognizing the inter-existence of all life forms.

CO-ARISING OF BODY AND MIND

The processes of our mind can seem more real to us than anything else, allowing our thoughts to be taken as more worthy and reliable than the material realm in which we are embedded. When this happens, as it does in most religious traditions of the patriarchal era, a split occurs, weakening our relation to the natural world and the wisdom of our own bodies. The Buddha warned us against this and took pains to illuminate the radical interdependence of mind and matter.

This is important, because the environmental crisis of our time has deep attitudinal roots. The bulldozing of nature and the abuse of our own bodies reveal the split in the psyche that cuts us off from the physical world. This separation engenders a fear of nature as well as a compulsion to control it. To fill the emptiness caused by this perceived separation, we seek satisfaction with passing diversions, be they alcohol, tobacco, drugs, or shopping.

What ways of thinking can help us come home again to the physical world? Marxism, capitalism, and classical science offer little help in healing the separation, because their materialism gives no weight to subjective experience.

When we turn instead to major theistic religious traditions, we find the same split—a stifling dichotomy between matter and mind. Behind their theologies and symbol systems, we detect a revulsion against the flesh. As I became acquainted with Buddhism and experienced the luminous beauty of its teachings about the mind, I began to wonder what the Dharma had to say about the body. Did it accord reality and dignity to the physical? Was it free of contempt for matter?

In ancient India, too, there were contending schools of thought as to the relation of mind and body. The materialists reduced mind to matter, and the Vedantans reduced matter to mind. The Buddha, taking a different approach, did not explain one in terms of the other or question the reality of either. Instead, he showed how they co-arise in interaction.

Here is an early image he and his followers used for the relation of mind to body, remembering that "name-and-form" was an early term for the physical body:

> . . . two sheaves of reeds leaning one against the other. Even so, friend, name-and-form comes to pass conditioned by consciousness, consciousness conditioned by name-and-form. . . . If, friend, I were to pull towards me one of those sheaves of reeds, the other would fall; if I were to pull towards me the other, the former would fall.[3]

This teaching can be puzzling to those of us familiar with ascetic passages in the early scriptures and practices for cultivating disdain of the body. But the body was never dismissed as less real or less valuable than consciousness, reason, or intellect. As the monks were to meditate on the impermanent and composite nature of the body, so were they also to meditate on the transient and composite nature of the mind.

Mind, too, was dissected and viewed in terms of the passing flux of thoughts, impulses, perceptions, and sensations of which it is constituted. No essence was held up as inherently nobler, purer, or more real than this bag of decaying flesh. In reflecting on the body, the monks' goal was to become more mindful of it, not to withdraw from it. The ascetic flavor of the early Buddhist texts should not mislead us. Never is matter presented as inherently dangerous or less real than consciousness.

Pleasures of the flesh that stimulate our craving are to be shunned, but so are rigid views and judgments of the mind. Indeed, the body is more innocent than our mental attachments. Of the four kinds of craving described in the Mahanidana Sutra, "grasping at sense objects . . . speculative opinions . . . rule and ritual . . . theories of the soul"—only one is physical.[4] Only one involves sense desire or bodily appetite.

LARGER BODY, LARGER MIND

If consciousness co-arises with form, can we limit it to the human realm? Is it the unique possession of our species? Does it set us apart from the rest of life? The Dharma says no. Consciousness pervades all existence. That teaching can begin to free us from the anthropocentrism we have inherited from the Abrahamic religions and Western philosophical thought.

The English-born monk and scholar Sangharakshita notes that in Buddhism, the human is but "one manifestation of a current of psycho-physical energy, manifesting now as god, now as animal, etc."[5] He points out that this belief in psychic continuity underlies the compassion for other creatures, the "boundless heart" that the Buddha exemplified.

Consciousness is throughout, but it is not unitary. It is not some universal essence or glue—the eternal oneness we find in Hinduism. There, the omnipresence of Brahman or the pervasiveness of Vishnu remains changeless and eternal behind the screen of illusion, or *maya*. To gain awareness of this supernal consciousness, one must strip away the material particularities of life's forms. But in the Buddhadharma, where consciousness co-arises with form, it is, in every instance, particular. It is characterized not by sameness, but by its own unique presence, its "thatness" or "suchness," called *tathata* in Sanskrit.

Our minds can open to connection with all life forms and learn from them, as the Buddha did from his earlier incarnations as elephant, rabbit, serpent, and many others. Not only seers and shamans, but scientists also have revealed the capacity of the human spirit to know and be informed by its connectedness to other life forms. This is a gift and saving grace.

The Dharma vision of a co-arising world, alive with consciousness, is a powerful inspiration for the healing of the Earth. It helps us see two important things. First, it shows us how profoundly we're imbedded in the web of life, thus relieving us of our human arrogance and loneliness. Second, it frees us from having to have it all figured out ahead of time, for options arise as we walk the path and meet each other on the road.

BODY/MIND IN SYSTEMS THINKING

Like Buddhism, systems thinking and philosophy recognizes that consciousness is endemic to the universe, immanent in all life forms. This pervasiveness of mind is articulated by systems thinkers in a variety of ways. For example, Gregory Bateson refers to "the pattern that connects" in the flow of information or feedback loops that interweave living systems, and Ervin Laszlo speaks of the "interiority" of living systems: "The phenomenon of mind is neither an intrusion into the cosmos from some outside agency, nor the emergence of something out of nothing. Mind is but the internal aspect of the connectivity of systems within the matrix. . . . The mind as knower is continuous with the rest of the universe as known. Hence in this metaphysics there is no gap between subject and object. . . . These terms refer to arbitrarily abstracted entities."[6]

Natural systems are both physical and mental. When we observe them (that is, from outside), says Laszlo, we perceive them as physical. When they experience themselves, which is their subjectivity, that is mind. Mind and body then are two perspectives of the same phenomenon, and you cannot reduce one to the other. Like the inside and outside of a coat or a brain, the two aspects are both inseparable and mutually exclusive. And they correspond to each other in complexity—the subjective experience of a cell would be correspondingly simple, and it would be hard for a brain to imagine that is composed of a hundred billion cells. As Laszlo says, its "mind-events must be entirely different in 'feel' from ours, yet they can be mind-events nevertheless, i.e., types of sensations correlated with, but different from physical processes."[7] Mind is the subjectivity of any system experiencing itself.

One way in which a nerve cell's "mind" would be different in "feel" is that it does not loop back on itself in the complexity of circuits that are required to plan ahead and make decisions. Self-reflexive consciousness evolved as the system grew so complex in its organization and behaviors that it could no longer self-regulate automatically or on instinct alone. Feedback about feedback, in assemblies of loops, had to be consciously monitored. We watch what we do, and decide.

We exist in nested hierarchies of natural systems, from the molecules and organs that comprise our bodies to the social systems and ecosystems that sustain us from without. Neither the systems inside us nor the systems around us have this self-reflexive consciousness. That capacity to think and choose requires a high degree of internal differentiation and a high degree of integration found in highly evolved organisms.

Considering what humans are doing to their world, our use of self-reflexive consciousness is not very encouraging. But the story is not finished. Throughout time, systems continue to self-organize and evolve, and new levels of systemic mind can emerge. They can emerge as we work together, in synergy toward common goals, weaving new neural assemblies and feedback circuits. Sometimes, as I behold the ways we attune and support each other in cooperative efforts on behalf of Earth, I imagine that we ourselves are like nerve cells in a larger brain—and that brain is starting to think.

As we take part in the healing of our world, we are supported by the co-arising universe itself. Life pulses through its mind-body, taking countless forms to accompany and teach us. They exist within us in the beautiful homeostatic systems of lymph and blood; they surround us in the ecosystems of swamp and forest and in the social systems of our neighborhoods and *sanghas*. We don't have to go it alone, and we can't. The strength and wisdom we need is not to be concocted on our own, but to be found in interaction—for that is how they arise, interdependently.

The same is true for our goals and the visions that guide us; they, too, interdependently co-arise. New visions do not come from blueprints inside our heads, concocted by past experience and old habits of thinking, so much as from our interactions with our world and fresh sensations and perceptions. And for that we need Earth and body, the stuff out of which we are made. For these remind us that we are not brains on the end of a stick, but an organic, integral part of the web of life. Matter

itself, if we attend to it mindfully and gratefully, can help liberate us from delusion. After all, it is mind, not matter, that is in
bondage.

Indeed, the particularity of matter, the thingness of things,
is helpful to the mind in returning it to the immediacy of experience. For it is not through its fancies, delusory as they can
be, or through the concepts to which it tenaciously clings, that
mind is illumined. It is through attention to the here and now,
to what eludes its fabrications, that mind can overleap its self-
enclosing constructs and perceive the living process of which
it is a part.

SIX

THE CO-ARISING OF
KNOWER AND KNOWN

In the most essential way we are citizens of the
great nature of infinite contingency.

—ELIZABETH NAMGYEL

Is the world as I perceive it? Or am I making it up? These eternal
questions bemuse the mind of the growing child and of citizens
confronting propaganda or given cause to think the press or
government or social media are deceiving them.

In debating the relative reality of perceiver and perceived,
mainstream Western thought has tended to place stress exclu-
sively on one or the other. Classical empiricists hold that the
world gives rise to what we perceive; its data are registered
passively on our neutral sense organs. These data are taken as
"given," unquestionably present, just like the world.

And, of course, there are those thinkers and traditions that
have disagreed. Fascinated by the power of mind, subjective
idealists consider external phenomena as largely projections.
In this view, consciousness is primary and independent of the
impressions it receives.

These two positions, still vying for allegiance in our day, were vigorously debated in ancient India, during the Buddha's life. Instead of taking sides, Gautama opened a third alternative. He taught that knower and known, perceiver and perceived, arise interdependently.

This teaching is important for us to grasp as we free ourselves from the reductionism of classical science, where only external phenomena are seen as really real. Without it, we can easily flip over into the opposite and equally one-sided extreme. We can imagine that the world we see is only a projection of our minds and that we create it unilaterally.

PERCEIVING AND KNOWING

It's worth noting that the Buddha took pains to distinguish his teachings from those of the Upanishads, which were foundational to Vedic and subsequent Hindu thought. In those important traditions, all perception and knowing are the function of the Atman, an eternal, universal Self at the core of one's being. "There is no other seer than he, no other hearer than he."[1] The Atman is the silent witness, the imperturbable rider of the chariot, spectator of all events.

In contrast, the Buddha taught that perceiving and knowing are interactive; they happen through a convergence of factors. Like a fire that cannot burn without the wood or dried grass on which it feeds, all consciousness requires an object. Here sensory perception does not reside in the power of a single agent, but rather in the interaction of three conditions: (1) a sense organ, (2) a sense object coming within its range, and (3) contact between the two. These conditions, especially the first two, constitute the sphere or gateway (*ayatana*) through which perception occurs.

While consciousness conditions the gateway through which perception occurs, it is conditioned, in turn, by the objects perceived. It is ignited by them, like a flame. As the Buddha explained,

> Monks, as a fire burns because of this or that appropriate condition, by that it is known: if a fire burns because of sticks, it is known as a stick fire . . . and if a fire burns because of grass, it is known as a grass fire. . . . Even so, monks, when consciousness arises because of eye and material shapes, it is known as visual consciousness. . . . When consciousness arises because of mind and mental objects, it is known as mental consciousness.[2]

Consciousness co-arises with sensory activity. It does not exist independently but is ignited into being, conditioned by its object. It is always consciousness *of* something. The passage concludes, "Apart from condition, there is no origination of consciousness."[3]

Because he did not see consciousness as existing prior to or independently of the world it knows, the Buddha rejected a priori reasoning. He posited no realm of pure logic aloof from the sensory world. "There exist," he said, "no diverse truths which in the world are eternal, apart from perception." Views arrived at and defended in terms of pure reason alone are suspect in the Buddhist view, because knowing is conditioned by habit and vested interests. The Buddha made this clear: "Were a man to say: I shall show the coming, the going, the passing away, the arising, the growth, the increase or development of consciousness apart from body, sensation, perception and volitional formations, he would be speaking about something which does not exist."[4]

The "volitional formations," called *sankhara* in the original Pali, are the habits and tendencies generated by previous activity. They load our sense impressions with the freight of past experiences and associations. The series of causal factors used in the teaching of paticca samuppada shows how the sankhara shape cognition and how, in turn, perceptions and feelings arise. With feelings of attraction or aversion, ego consciousness arises. There is the sense of something to defend or enhance. And the imagined needs of the ego proceed to impose fabrications on the external world. We see the world through filters upon filters of time, culture, race, class, gender, and a host of other subjective and social identities.

Perception, then, is a highly interpretive process. We create our worlds, but we do not do so unilaterally, for consciousness is conditioned by that upon which it feeds; subject and object are interdependent. The Buddha denied neither the "thereness" of the sense objects nor the projective capacities of the mind; he simply saw the process as a two-way street. The conditioning is mutual.

INFORMATION LOOPS

In our own day, general systems theory gives us conceptual tools for understanding this interaction between knower and known. In the systems view, cognitive activity is seen as a circuit that embraces both the external world and that which perceives it.

Open systems, including cognitive systems like our minds, maintain and organize themselves by virtue of feedback—that is, by monitoring their interactions with their environment. *Monitoring* is a key term in systems theory. All open systems self-monitor; it is like a naturally occurring mindfulness. That is how our blood and the oceans, for example, regulate levels of salinity. They watch what is happening and adjust. They do this by a process of matching—matching the observed results of behavior with inner pre-established goals. It is feedback that just told me to rewrite a sentence because it inaccurately conveyed the meaning I intended. It is feedback that kept my son's car on the road this afternoon as he drove me home. Instant by instant, so constantly that it is usually unconscious, we proceed by *steering*—which is the root meaning of *cybernetics*.

Feedback creates causal circuits or loops of knowing. In these information circuits, our perceptions are conditioned by previous experience. In other words, we see by interpreting, and each of us lives in our own assumed form-world. The memories, expectations, and habits carried forward from the past infuse and give shape to our perceptions. They develop internal codes and constructs by which we order and filter the influx of raw data.

The codes and constructs we use to interpret our world are functional equivalents to the Buddhist notion of sankhara, volitional formations or impulses. The modern monk-scholar Bhikkhu Analayo calls sankhara, "the ruts and grooves of our mental terrain." He says that they influence every moment of our lived experience. While the Buddhist view highlights the role of attachment in the perpetuation of these formations, both bodies of thought recognize the role codes play in perception, and both see them as subject to alteration. Formed by experience, these codes are modified by experience.

Our preconceptions not only shape our interpretations of the world but impinge on the world itself. For feedback loops extend beyond the subjective realm and circle through the environment "out there." To see how world and mind shape each other, let us look at two main ways feedback works. One is through *homeostatic* (or negative) feedback, by which the world around us is brought into line with our own assumptions and goals. The other, through *adaptive* (or positive) feedback, leads to change in the internal codes themselves. Popular usage of the terms *negative feedback* and *positive feedback* reverses their meaning in systems thinking, where negative feedback indicates you are on track, with no need for adjustment, and positive feedback signals a deviation from one's objective and the need to correct or alter course.

By the first kind of feedback, we act upon our environment to make it intelligible in terms of our inner pictures and ideas. In this way, we are said to "project" our codes upon the environment so that it will continue to confirm our expectations and serve our goals. By such projection, scientists shape their research to yield the kinds of data that can fit their hypotheses, and architects design buildings to give form to their dreams. To perpetuate the match between perception and expectation, we impose shapes on our world, which then reflects them back. In excavated gardens or fortifications, we can read something of the character of an ancient city, for in them, its meanings, values, and constructs took form. Notions incarnate. And when we possess a powerful technology, this incarnational capacity is fearsome. Our imaginations erect Pentagons and Disneylands, and even the land itself mirrors back our fantasies. Gouged and paved over, it testifies to our search for mastery—and our fear of what we cannot control. In the world we create, we encounter ourselves.

The second type of feedback, called *adaptive* or *positive feedback*, occurs when there is a persistent mismatch between perception and code—that is, when we can no longer interpret experience in terms of our old assumptions. The cognitive system then searches for new codes by which novel and confusing perceptions can be understood and even resolved. This search amounts to an exploration of new ways to reorganize itself—and it continues until codes and constructs evolve that can deal with the new data.

Thus do living systems adapt by transforming themselves, and thus does learning happen. Real learning is not something added; it is a reorganization of the system. New nets and assemblies occur, loops form, alternate pathways develop. The viewed world is different, and so is the viewer. When, in the sixteenth and seventeenth centuries, Copernicus and Kepler produced compelling evidence that the Earth revolved around the sun, it was not just additional information. A revolution occurred in our experience of the world and in the ways we see and think. Now, in our own time, the Gaia theory—that Earth itself is a living system—calls for a comparable transformation in our understanding of our world and of ourselves.

We recognize here the creative function of cognitive crisis. When old, habitual modes of interpretation become dysfunctional, it can be painful and disorienting—a dark night of the soul. That kind of confusion, however, is usually fruitful. It motivates the system to self-organize in more inclusive ways, embracing and integrating data of which it had been previously unaware.

A Zen master, approached for teachings, filled his caller's tea cup till it overflowed—showing, in this manner, that the new could not be perceived until one has emptied oneself of preconceived notions. Similarly, the Buddha did not pour pronouncements into his followers' heads, so much as invite them to free themselves of habitual ways of seeing.

Seen in systems terms, the practice of *vipassana*, or insight meditation, represents a short-circuiting of the codes and constructs we impose upon reality. These are undercut as the mind trains to register perceptions without editorial comment or discursive thought. The application of bare attention allows us to step aside from the mental chatter that perpetuates our preconceptions. Rather than eliminating noise to extract message, the meditator switches off the message in order to attend to the noise. The exercise amounts to a deliberate mismatching, or production, of positive feedback, as awareness widens to the rush of impersonal psycho-physical events, wherein the habitual "I" is no longer discernible. Bare attention to the flow of experience yields no experiencer separable from the flow, and the Buddha's teaching about the self becomes more than a theory. The absence of a permanent, separate self can erupt as a reality that changes the face of life.

If knowing is interactive, any pursuit of final certainty or claim to absolute truth is doomed. For all knowing is relative to the perspective of the knower and is conditioned by their past experience.

The Buddha was unique among teachers of his time in refusing to make definitive statements on metaphysical matters. To the exasperation of many of his followers, he refused to speculate on topics that are not subject to direct, personal experience, such as the existence of a creator or the reality of an afterlife. Theories that define the ultimate source and status of things were suspect, because they are of necessity partial, and also because they become objects of attachment. Views that claimed exclusive and final accuracy were shunned and dismissed by the Buddha: "Whatever is esteemed as truth by other folk, amidst those who are entrenched in their own views . . . I hold none as true or false. This barb I beheld well in advance, whereon mankind is hooked, impaled: 'I know, I see, 'tis verily so'—no such clinging for the Tathagatas."[5]

I love this sly and pithy observation. He does not say they are wrong, who assert, "I know, I see, 'tis verily so." He just says that they are hooked, that they are not free. And he is glad not to be hooked himself—"no such clinging for the Tathagatas" (another word for Buddhas).

The quote reminds me of Dr. Sri Ariyaratne, founder of Sarvodaya, the Buddhist-inspired community development movement in Sri Lanka. One day I accompanied Ari, as he is called by his friends, on a visit to a Sarvodaya rural center, and we ran across a Western guru in robes who preached to us the whole time, serenely oozing his certitude of ultimate truth. When Ari and I got back in the car, I vented my irritation at the pompous fellow, pointing out emphatically how wrong he was. Ari just laughed and said, "Looks like he's 'impaled on the barb.' But you don't need to be!"

The impossibility of arriving at ultimate formulations of reality does not represent a defeat for the inquiring mind. So long as we claim no authority beyond our own experience, what we speak has the ring of truth. It is only final assertions that are suspect, not the process of knowing itself, for we each have a valid and important perspective on what is. And to the extent that we can acknowledge the partiality of this perspective, what we say and believe stays clear and true.

SEVEN

KARMA:
THE CO-ARISING OF
DOER AND DEED

We build the road and the road builds us.

—SARVODAYA MOVEMENT IN SRI LANKA

The Buddha's teaching of *anatta,* that there is no separate and permanent self, is a keystone to the Dharma. When I began to register the meaning of this teaching, I felt a tremendous release. I sensed how it could liberate me from habits of self-concern. It promised freedom to act—freedom to do what is to be done, without endlessly taking my spiritual and psychological pulse before getting on with it.

I received early lessons in anatta from my first meditation teacher, Sister Karma Khechog Palmo, also known as Freda Bedi, an English-born Tibetan Buddhist nun in India. On my retreat at her nunnery, which she'd established for Tibetan refugees, she came to my room to see how I was doing. When I made statements such as "I cannot sit still" or "I'm lazy" or "I'm restless," she would immediately cut me short. "Stop!" she'd say, "Stop saying 'I' in that way, when talking about your experience." Such "I" statements work like cement, lending a kind of permanence to passing feelings. Sister Palmo pointed out that it is more accurate to say, "impatience is happening" or "fears are arising."

Her admonishments helped me recognize the burden of a solidified self, and the burden began to lift. The "Joanna" who kept looking in the mirror to check her rightness or worthiness or guilt seemed to dissolve a little.

But the teaching of anatta can seem, at first approach, to free us from conventional morality as well. A young woman I knew, who had been recently exposed to Buddhist ideas, was leaving a hotel after a conference when her suitcase fell open. Along with her clothes and cosmetics, a set of the hotel's towels spilled out on the lobby floor. With an embarrassed shrug, she handed the towels to the bellboy and proceeded out the door. Her horrified roommate asked her if she wasn't ashamed of herself. "What self?" she said. "You only get uptight about this if you believe in the self. At least I'm free of *that* illusion."

Her comment may sound blithe or silly, but it highlights an issue in Buddhist thought that has been problematic for many. What is there to get uptight about if we are but a passing flow of psychophysical events? Does it matter what we do? Are we accountable for our acts? These questions have puzzled some Buddhist scholars too, especially in the West. Pointing out apparent contradictions between the doctrine of anatta and the ethical exhortations of the Buddha, a number have concluded that it weakens any notion of personal accountability.

The basic issue here is the connection between what we do and what we are. If we think of what we do in terms of our participation in the web of life, the question is whether and how our action affects that participation—that is, our capacity to know, choose, and enjoy. If not, then notions of responsibility are tangential to one's life, noble but inconsequential. If they do, then distinctions between the pragmatic and the moral dissolve. In the perspective of interdependent co-arising, this is the case. What we do not only matters, it *molds* us.

THE TEACHING OF KARMA

The concept of *karma* is often associated with belief in rebirth or reincarnation, a belief that was almost universally accepted in the culture of the Buddha's time. Many questions addressed to the Buddha concerning the course of the spiritual life, and particularly the moral effect of deeds, were posed within the context of this widely held belief. The teaching of no-self raised problems: If the self is transient, how can it survive from one life to the next? And how can it be affected by previous lives?

Actually, the Buddha did not consider it useful to reflect on the possibility and character of other lifetimes. He said that if you really understand this causal law, you won't run back to the past, thinking: "Did I live in times gone by? Or did I not? What was I in times gone by? How was I then? Or free from being what, did I become what?" Nor will you run toward the future, thinking: "Shall I be reborn in a future time, or shall I not? What shall I become in the future?" As he concluded, "These questions never arise, brethren, if by right insight [you] see things as they really are, both this causal happening and things as having causally happened"—a clear affirmation of paticca samuppada.[1]

Yet, even focusing on this present incarnation, disciples often queried the Buddha as to who is responsible for the habits, sufferings, and pleasures we experience. One cannot say, he would reply, that "one and the same person both acts and experiences the result," for the person is different, altered. There *is* continuity, but it inheres in the reflexive dynamics of action, shaping that which brought it forth.

The term *karma* is generally used to mean "action." Early on, in pre-Buddhist literature, the word denoted ritual acts; then, by extension, it meant religiously ordained social duties. In the Buddhist texts, it is broadened to include all volitional behavior—bodily, verbal, and mental. This is what we are. As Pali scholar T. W. Rhys Davids points out, "Where others said 'soul,' Gautama usually said 'action.'"[2]

The effect of our behavior is inescapable, not because God watches and tallies, or an angel marks our acts in a ledger, but because our acts co-determine what we become. They do so by means of the volitional formations. These habits and inclinations condition the ways in which we interpret and react to things. The term *sankhara* means "put together," "compounded." Sankharas accrue from previous volitional acts and represent the reflexive or recoil effects of these actions—the tendencies they create, the habits they perpetuate.

Because the character of a person's experience is affected by these formations, their identity is inseparable from what they do and think, and have done and thought. They are neither aloof from these acts nor their victim. They are their identity, continuity, and resource, as the Anguttara Nikaya declares.

> My action is my possession,
> my action is my inheritance,
> my action is the womb which bears me,
> my action is my refuge.[3]

LIBERATION OF THE WILL

By recognizing the creative interaction between past and present, the Buddha's view of karma diverged from the more highly deterministic notions of karma current in his time. The Jains, for example, taught that every single act, regardless of its motivation or circumstance, inexorably bears its fruit. No spiritual progress can be made without personally undergoing all the consequences. Set in motion by the physical effects of deeds, karma represents a kind of substance or film, an obscuring accumulation that only can be worn away through expiation. This process of wearing away can be hastened by mortification of the flesh. The Ajivika view, also taught in the Buddha's time, is even more deterministic. Considering *every* aspect of present experience—mental and physical—as the result of past action, it sees any human effort whatever as fruitless.

If karma cannot be changed, the Buddha said, "all effort is fruitless." This he would not allow. He rejected determinist views of karma because of their crippling effect on human will. They provide, he said, "neither the desire to do, nor the effort to do, nor the necessity to do this deed or abstain from that deed. So then, the necessity for action or inaction [is] not found to exist in truth or verity."[4] This "desire to do, and effort to do"—in other words, our volition—modifies the effects of our past and broadens the scope for present endeavor. This emphasis on will is the most distinctive feature of the Buddhist concept of karma. The Buddha said, "Where there have been deeds, Ananda, personal weal and woe are in consequence of the will there was in the deeds."[5]

That is why the sankharas, which condition our perceptions and cognitions, are understood as "volitional formations."
Shaped by our desires, they carry forward the energy of the
will. The power inherent in past acts resides in the choices that
produced them.

A human existence is considered to be incomparably precious because intention is so important and choice so con-
sequential. Beings in other realms of the wheel of life, such
as animals, ghosts, and gods, experience pain and pleasure,
but only human beings are understood as capable of making
choices. Given the astronomical number of other forms of life,
this human opportunity is seen as extraordinarily rare and
valuable.

Since will determines the effect of acts, for good or for grief,
it must be mobilized. Exertion is required. The early scriptures
abound in exhortations to vigorous effort. Those who would
"rise up from what is unskilled and establish [themselves] in
what is skilled," Buddhist practitioners are summoned repeatedly by the scriptures to be "intent on vigilance," and "of stirred
up energy, self-resolute, with mindfulness aroused."[6] One of
the cardinal obstacles is *thinamiddham*, "sloth" or "lethargy."
By the same token, *viriya* (understood as "energy," "resolution,"
or "vigor") is seen as essential to enlightenment and a cardinal
virtue in its own right. This energy is in vivid contrast to the
passivity and fatalism popularly associated with the notion of
karma. Here will is primary, and it can be trained: "Wherefore,
brethren, thus must ye train yourselves: liberation of the will
through love we will develop, we will often practice it, we will
make it a vehicle and a base, take our stand upon it, store it up,
thoroughly set it going."[7]

In the early Buddhist view, then, a person's identity resides not in an enduring self but in their actions, that is, in the choices that shape these actions. Because the dispositions formed by previous choices can be modified, in turn, by present behavior, one's identity as choice-maker is fluid, one's experience alterable. Affected by the past, one's identity can also break free of the past.

A SYSTEMS VIEW OF KARMA

Systems thinking has helped me understand the Buddha's view of karma. Both bodies of thought see that what we do shapes who we are. Because the open system is self-organizing, its behavior cannot be dictated from without. External pressures can do no more than interact with the system's internal organization. A person's actions derive from their unique observations and reflections; unfolding circumstances bring ever new perceptions, conditions, and opportunities.

As political scientist Karl Deutsch says, in reference to the self-organizing of a conscious system: "Thanks to what it has learned in the past, it is not wholly subject to the present. Thanks to what it still can learn, it is not wholly subject to the past. Its internal rearrangements in response to each new challenge are made by the interplay between its present and its past."[8]

Meta-level reflections arise, bringing awareness of other choices that could be made, and because they do, the individual "could always have acted otherwise." Deutsch goes on to say: "Each of us is responsible for what he is now, for the personality he himself has acquired by his past actions. . . . Nor are we wholly prisoners of any one decision or any one experience. Ordinarily, it takes many repetitions so to stock a mind with memories and habits that at long last lead to the same city, whether it be taken, in religious language, as the City of Destruction, or the City of Salvation."[9]

One is struck by the parallels to the Buddhist idea of karma and especially the sankharas—the memories and habits that "stock the mind." The systems view, like the Buddhist view, does not see us as victims of our past, hapless pawns of forces and times beyond our reach; rather, as Deutsch continues: "It sees in the actual moment of decision only a denouement in which we reveal to ourselves and to others what we have already become thus far. Each step on the road to 'heaven' or to 'hell,' to harmonious autonomy or to disintegration, was marked by a free decision. . . . The determinate part of our behavior is the stored result of our past free decisions."[10]

Choice is so important because it actually constitutes what it means to be a person. To systems psychologist O. H. Mowrer, choice defines consciousness itself. "The eternal question is, 'What to do? How to act?' And consciousness, as I conceive it, is the operation whereby information is continuously received, evaluated and summarized in the form of 'decisions,' 'choices,' 'intentions.'"[11]

Through the operation of feedback, the behaviors we adopt and the goals we pursue take root in the psyche. They affect the ways we interpret experience, and these ways constitute who we are. Doer and deed co-arise. Hence our continuity of character, bearing the stamp of repeated choice and habit. Hence also our freedom, for new options arise with each present act of will.

Here then is the answer to our question, "Does it matter what we do?" It matters to the extent that *we* matter. Indeed, our acts matter—incarnate—in us, for they make us what we are. Though we fall into feelings of overwhelm or hopelessness, we can still choose to see what is possible.

This spells both grief and promise for the self we tend to posit and on whose behalf we tend to act. Because it is altered by each act, wise or foolish, fearful or brave, the self, even as decision maker, is doomed as an enduring entity. Constantly changing, it arises and passes. Yet in that very evanescence lies promise. For in the flow of perception and response, choices can be made that open broader vistas to perceive and know, wider opportunities to love and to act.

EIGHT

THE CO-ARISING OF SELF AND SOCIETY

The master's tools will never dismantle the master's house.

—AUDRE LORDE

After supper at a rural community center, half a dozen visitors stood and talked by the fire. We had enjoyed a delicious meal of fresh home-grown produce. Conversation turned to our lives in the city and the lack of easy access to food that is not irradiated, adulterated with additives, or contaminated with pesticides. In many low-income neighborhoods there is little to no access to healthy food at all. We shared our discouragement.

A woman who had quietly joined our group and listened to our tales spoke up. "The best thing to do," she said, "is take control of your own life. Leave the polluted air of the city. Drink pure spring water. Eat produce that you have grown yourself or know firsthand is safe." She said, firmly, "That's all we can do now, take care of ourselves."

I listened to her attentively, hearing the logic of her statement. The urban activists among us had adopted it to some extent, installing water-purifying systems in our kitchens, shopping at farmers' markets, and subscribing to community-supported agriculture programs (CSAs) that deliver fresh-from-the-farm fruits and vegetables to your door. But her logic made curious our efforts to change the status quo and challenge our institutions. She, in contrast, seemed to believe that she could separate herself from society and declare independence from the world at large.

Once again, the Buddha's teaching of interdependent co-arising arose in my mind. I groped in vain for a simple comment that could convey the nature of our relationship to the institutions of our society, an interexistence so real that we cannot escape it by going to live in the country and growing our own food.

The institutions of our society co-arise with us. They are not independent structures separate from our inner lives, like some backdrop to our personal dramas. Nor are they mere projections or reflections of our own minds. As collective forms of our ignorance, fears, and greed, they acquire their own momentum, enlist our widespread collusion, and depend on our mutual consent.

Poring over early Buddhist scriptures, I appreciated the novelty of these teachings, and their daring. I found many passages where the Buddha describes the interdependence of self and society, and its implications for our political and economic behavior.

The prevailing view of things in the Buddha's time was very different. The dominant Brahmanic worldview saw social systems as preordained, divinely created at the beginning of our world. The institution of caste, for example, embodies the cosmic act by which the godhead in the form of the *Mahapurusha*, the Primordial Person, created the world out of his vast body. From his head, trunk, and limbs issued the major caste divisions. Hence the divine right of kings, the innate role of priests, and the fixed, subordinate functions of the lower castes.

In radical contrast to this view, the Buddha saw all social structures as impermanent, contingent products of human interaction, reflecting the law of interdependent co-arising. He illustrated this in the Aggañña Sutta, a discourse so popular that it resurfaces again and again in canonical and post-canonical writings and even in the preamble to the first Burmese constitution. In this genesis story, he recounts the origins of institutions as they reflect human behavior. As you read the summary of the sutra below, bear in mind that the Buddha didn't intend it to be taken literally but more to illustrate reciprocal causality. The Buddha was also challenging metaphysical conjectures that claimed to know the ultimate source of all things.

A BUDDHIST CREATION STORY

In the beginning of a world cycle, neither beings nor their world had solid form or distinctive features. Weightless, luminous, and identical, the beings wafted about over a dark and watery expanse. When a frothy substance appeared on the waters, they tasted it. It was delicious, and for its sweet honey flavor a craving arose.

As the beings consumed more and more, both they and their world changed, becoming more distinct. The beings began to lose their identical luminosity, and as they did, the sun, moon, and stars appeared, bringing with them the alternation of day and night. The beings began to solidify and vary in appearance.

Pride and vanity arose as they compared their beauty, and the savory froth vanished. The beings bewailed its loss: "Ah, the savor of it!" In its place, on an earth that was now firmer, mushroom-like growths appeared of similar tastiness—only to disappear as the creatures fattened on them and changed form again. The mushrooms were replaced by vines, and these, in turn, by rice.

With every new growth, the beings craved and ate, growing more substantial and diverse. At each stage, their use of the natural world further modified it, engendering more solidity and new forms of vegetation, and with such usage they themselves changed, developing more and more distinctive features. In this interaction both creatures and world progressively differentiated, each gaining in solidity and variety.

When the rice first grew, it was without husk and, after being harvested, would grow again in a day. A lazy person, to save effort, decided to harvest enough for two meals at once. Soon all beings were harvesting for two days at a time, then four days, then eight. With this new practice of hoarding, the rice changed: a husk appeared around the grain, and the cut stem did not grow again. It stood only as dry stubble. So the people divided and fenced the land, setting boundaries to ensure their private source of food.

Then a few greedy people took some rice from their neighbor's plot. Admonished by the others, they promised to refrain, but then they took more rice again, and again. Since admonishment did not stop them, they were beaten. With the institution of private property, theft arose and also lying and abuse and violence.

Soon such acts were so rampant and the situation so chaotic that the people decided to select one of their own to act on their behalf and to receive, in return for this service, a portion of rice. So arose the *Mahasammata*, the great elected one, and with his rule, order prevailed. Such is the origin of kingship and the warrior class; and so, by the assumption and differentiation of roles, did the other major divisions of society evolve—the Brahmins, Vaisyas, and Sudras.

A RECIPROCAL SOCIAL CONTRACT

My interest here is to stress the profound connection with the doctrine of interdependent co-arising. Class and caste were not established by divine fiat; they developed from the interactions of beings like ourselves. They were circumstantial in origin. Within that mutual causal perception of reality, one is not a self-existent being, nor are the institutions of society eternally fixed. They are mutable and they mirror our greeds, as does, indeed, the face of nature itself. Co-arising with our actions, they, like us, can be changed by our actions. As our own dynamic processes can be transformed, so can they.

This creation story is said to be the first expression in Indian political thought of a theory of social contract. Government began with the people, as a result of their banding together by choice. The Mahasammata was not divinely appointed and anointed but was chosen by peers to act in their stead and serve their purposes. The kind of causality at play here shows how different the Buddhist concept is from the Western notion of social contract associated with Locke and Rousseau. In the Western concept, individuals who band together to create institutions remain basically unaltered by their association. In interdependent co-arising, however, self, society, and world are *all* reciprocally changed by their interactions and are, in turn, conditioned by them.

The causal dynamics conveyed in the Agganna Sutta underlie the Buddha's social, economic, and political teachings. They are basic to his rejection of caste discrimination and the egalitarian composition of the Sangha; his distrust of private property and the establishment of voluntary poverty, sharing, and alms-begging in the Sangha; his advocacy of government by assembly and consensus; and the Sangha's rules for debate and the settlement of differences.

The Buddha acknowledged that discrimination and oppression shaped the scope and character of people's lives, but he never conceded that such conditions foreclosed their capacity to live nobly and achieve enlightenment. He delivered this teaching whenever he was questioned about the obvious diversity his Sangha displayed. Many well-born contemporaries were puzzled and even shocked that the Buddha welcomed into his order followers from all strata of society, including merchants, runaway soldiers, and slaves. Brahmin priests heaped "copious and characteristic abuse" on their peers who joined the Sangha and reviled the Sangha itself for opening its doors to "the vulgar rich, the swarthy skinned and the menials." As Jesus did, the Buddha saw pride in social rank as a spiritual obstacle. As he said in the Ambattha Sutta, "Whoever is in bondage to the notions of birth or lineage, or to pride in social position or connection by marriage, is far from wisdom and righteousness."[1]

POLITICAL PARTICIPATION

In contrast to the Brahmanical notion of a divinely predetermined and eternally valid system of government, the Buddha presented political institutions as human-made and transient,

subject to the law of interdependent co-arising. It is not surprising that unlike other wandering religious teachers of his
period, he often taught in cities, in the company of rulers, and
on the periphery of political power.

Gautama had grown up in a tribal republic to the north
of the two monarchies in which he taught. Such republics had
been self-governed by a council or assembly, called a *sangha*.
When, years later, he established his own monastic order, he
called it by the same name, Sangha. From the outset, it was
more of an alternative community than a retreat from the world.

The order arose, of course, as a vehicle for the transmission
of teachings and a locus for the restructuring of consciousness
through meditation. But it represented as well an embodiment
of social ideals. It served as a model for social equality, democratic process, and economic sharing. Inspired by the ancient
tribal councils, decisions in the new monastic order were made
by consensus, "in concord." Scriptural passages such as the following represent the first references in Indian history to rule
by assembly: "So long, O Bhikkhus, as the brethren foregather
often, and frequent the formal meetings of their Order—so
long as they meet together in concord, and rise in concord, and
carry out in concord the duties of the Order . . . so long may the
brethren be expected not to decline, but to prosper."[2]

Repression of beliefs was not to be tolerated, so a rule
of schism, or *sanghabheda*, was instituted, in which members
who disagreed with a sangha's emphasis or interpretation of the
teachings could simply form a new settlement within the larger
order. Within each settlement, select groups or committees,
each having its own jurisdiction and procedural rules, were
established to deal with matters administrative and doctrinal.

The expression of varying opinions in the *sanghakammas*, the assemblies for decision making, was facilitated by the taking of ballots (*salaka*), again the first recorded use of such procedure in the political history of India.

Since respect for alternative views was more important than ideological solidarity and centralized authority, the Sangha split into many schools. This proliferation of forms testifies to their strength and resilience. Given the endurance of the Buddhadharma over two and a half millennia, it would appear that it hardly required the centralized authority so often deemed necessary for the preservation of religion. Without a Rome or Jerusalem, Buddhism flowered in its diversity of forms, while repeatedly renewing, through study and action, its roots in the teachings of the Buddha.

ECONOMIC SHARING

In the Buddha's Dharma and Sangha, we see the kinds of economic concepts and practices that emerge when self and society are seen as interdependent. We see at work the values of non-attachment, generosity, and right livelihood.

The Buddha's teaching that suffering stems from craving (the Second Noble Truth) places a high value on self-restraint and low consumption. The traditional mendicant way of the monastic, modeled after the Buddha, embodies the conviction that freedom does not derive from wealth or the satisfaction of appetite. Liberation can be won from the insatiable greed to possess and consume and from the objects, thoughts, and habits that stimulate that wanting. Possessions, furthermore, are dangerous to the extent that they foster the notion of "mineness" (*mamatta*) and thus encourage belief in a permanent, separate self who possesses. In the Agganna Sutta, as we saw, the institution of private property is presented as the occasion for the arising of theft, lying, and violence. From this perspective, the goal of modern advertising, to induce the sensation of need and the desire to acquire, is immoral. For that matter, so is an economic system dependent on ever-widening public consumption of nonessential commodities and artifacts.

As an antidote to attachment and the delusion it engenders, the Buddha preached generosity (dana) and organized a community in which private property was renounced; all goods were shared in common. The sangha comprised, as its members, *bhikkhus* and *bhikkhunis*, terms which literally mean not "monks" and "nuns" but "sharesmen" and "shareswomen," those who receive a share of something. Their alms-begging was not just a handy means of subsistence. It was sacramental in nature, betokening relinquishment of personal wealth and trustful reliance on social relations.

The bhikkhus' relation to lay society was reciprocal and symbiotic. In return for material support, the monks and nuns provided counsel, delivered teachings, and exemplified the ideals they taught. They offered laypeople the opportunity to cultivate their own generosity through the giving of alms. In later centuries, the sangha's reciprocity included hospitals and orphanages maintained by the bhikkhus, as well as the erection of monuments, libraries, and universities. From the gifts it received, the sangha created a rich heritage of art and learning.

In the Buddha's teachings, economic sharing was held out as an ideal for relations between laypersons as well as bhikkhus; it was a prerequisite for a healthy society. While restraint in consumption was seen as salutary, the condition of poverty was not. The Buddha rejected mortification of the flesh and affirmed the rightful claims of this body "born of the great elements." Poverty tends to foment desire and attachment. As the Buddha said, a person cannot listen to the Dharma on an empty stomach.

In early Buddhism, there is no vicarious salvation. We are enjoined to be lamps unto ourselves. The responsibility of the individual to work out their own liberation requires an economics of sufficiency. An ideal social order, therefore, ensures that everyone has the necessary economic base for their spiritual development. An array of sutras and Jataka tales portray the wise ruler as engaging in broad public works and providing jobs, food, and shelter to the needy.

These scriptures express the economic interdependence between the state and its citizenry and the extent to which the state's health and security is a function of the well-being of all its people. When the king, in the Kutadanta Sutta, desires to offer a great ritual sacrifice to ensure his future welfare, he is reminded of lawless elements that trouble his realm, pillaging towns and making roads unsafe. His chaplain, who is identified as the Buddha himself in a former life, argues that neither fresh taxation nor punishment of the miscreants will end the disorder. The most effective solution is to create productive employment opportunities: give food and seed-corn to the farmers, capital to those who would engage in trade, and food and wages to those who would enter government service. Then "those men, following each his own business, will no longer harass the realm."[3] And, according to the story, not only did that happen, but with the advent of peace and security, the state's revenues increased.

In the Mahasudassana Sutta, the king "of greatest glory" is described and his magnificence is reflected in the facilities he creates for the comfort of his people. Many a Jataka tale presents the wise ruler as ministering to his realm in a similar fashion, offering resources that serve not only humans but beasts and birds as well. When the king is unrighteous, that seeps through society, infecting ministers and townspeople alike. Even the sun, moon, and stars go wrong in their course.

This concern for the commons was most notably demonstrated in the reign of the Buddhist king Ashoka. As his pillar and rock edicts attest, numerous public works were instituted: roads, wells, hostels, hospitals. "Moreover I have had banyan trees planted on the roads to give shade to man and beast; I have planted mango groves, and I have had ponds dug and shelters erected along the roads at every eight *kos* [roughly every fifteen miles]. Everywhere I have had wells dug for the benefit of man and beast. . . . What I have done has been done that man may conform to the Dharma."[4]

The inherent right to worthwhile work is reflected in the concept of "right livelihood," a practice focus of the Buddha's Eightfold Path. According to the teaching of interdependent co-arising, the work a person performs not only expresses their character but modifies it in turn. High value, therefore, must be placed on the nature of this work. Instead of being considered a necessary evil to which one is condemned, work is a vehicle for the creation and expression of our deepest values.

Meaningful employment is more important than the goods it produces. By linking people to their fellow beings in reciprocal relationship and enhancing their self-respect, the value of their work is beyond monetary measure. Labor policies and production plans that view work solely in terms of pay or profit degrade work and rob it of meaning. High wages, high dividends, increased production, or unemployment payments cannot compensate for the human loss that occurs when assembly-line production or joblessness deprive workers of developing and enjoying their skills.

ENDS AND MEANS

As has been repeatedly affirmed throughout human history, moral considerations pertain not only to the goals we try to achieve, but also to the manner in which we go about trying to achieve them. Frequently these appear at odds with each other, like the "war to end all wars." We all are familiar with the moral anguish that arises when worthy objectives seem attainable only by acts that appear to compromise them.

The conflict between ends and means arises from a dichotomized way of thinking, which leads us to imagine that the goal "out there" has an existence independent of ourselves or the methods we employ. Aristotle assumed this to be the case, when he explained his concept of final cause (*telos*). It is that for the sake of which one acts. In his *Nicomachean Ethics*, he said: "Wherever there are certain ends over and above the actions themselves, it is [their] nature . . . to be better than the activities."[5] The goal, then, appears as more real and more valuable than the activities leading to it; and these activities appear as merely instrumental to an end whose nature is more final and complete.

Such presuppositions lead to instrumentalist ways of thinking, where concern for ends overrides considerations of the ethical appropriateness of the means. Such considerations come to appear as moral niceties, welcome where they can be accommodated, but in the last analysis—when push comes to shove—the means are irrelevant to the goal in view, and more pragmatic choices prevail.

The dharma of interdependent co-arising turns this kind of thinking inside out. It asserts, as have many saints and teachers óver the ages, that the goal is not something "out there," aloof from our machinations, but rather, it is a function of the way itself, interdependent with our acts. As doer and deed are interconnected, as our own thoughts and actions are modified, so are our objectives. For however we articulate these objectives, they reflect our present perceptions and interpretations of reality, which are altered, however slightly, by every cognitive event. Means are not subordinate to ends so much as creative of them—they are ends-in-the-making. As Audre Lorde said, "The master's tools will never dismantle the master's house;" they can only perpetuate it.

The Buddha offered the Dharma not as a goal to be reached so much as a way (magga). Each step on this way is of intrinsic value, the Dharma being "glorious in the beginning, glorious in the middle, glorious at the end."[6] Value is intrinsic to each act because action (karma) is what we are and what we become. Although we are summoned to strive to transform our lives and our consciousness, we do so with the paradoxical knowledge that, though we may feel very far from where we want to be, there is no place to get to, for we are already there. This religious paradox, manifest in many faiths, overturns the problem of ends and means. It shows that the goals we pursue are not distant from us in time or space, but present realities, unfolding out of the core of our existence and capable of transforming in the moment.

We can never avoid what we seek to escape, least of all the political and economic institutions into which we are born. But by virtue of their dependence on our participation, by vote or speech, lobby or boycott, they can change. They mirror our truest intentions, values, and ideals. This is what I would have liked to say to the woman who joined us by the fire that night in the country, because it is what I hear the Buddha's teaching saying to me.

NINE

MOTHER OF ALL BUDDHAS

As Buddhas, world teachers
Compassionate, are your sons,
So you, O blessed one, are
Grandmother of all beings.
. . . He who sees you is liberated,
And he who does not see you is liberated, too.

—THE PERFECTION OF WISDOM IN 8,000 LINES

About five centuries after the Buddha, the Wheel of the Dharma, they say, turned again. The Buddha's central teaching of inter-dependent co-arising was confirmed and clothed in fresh language and imagery. This second turning of the wheel rings out in scriptures called Perfection of Wisdom, *Prajnaparamita*, which herald the advent of Mahayana Buddhism.

Here the hero figure of the bodhisattva appears, no longer solely identified with former lives of the Buddha, but with everyone who experiences the interdependent nature of reality. Here that wondrous insight is personified. Emerging in the same era as did her Mediterranean counterpart, Sophia, this embodiment of wisdom is female. She is the Perfection of Wisdom, the Mother of All Buddhas.

To get acquainted with her and learn more about the wisdom of interbeing, let us look at the richest of the scriptures honoring her, *The Perfection of Wisdom in 8,000 Lines*, written down between 100 BCE and 100 CE.

A DIFFERENT KIND OF WISDOM

The texts that bear her name are central to all major developments in later Buddhism, from Madhyamika philosophy to Vajrayana and Zen. These sutras reiterate her categorical difference from earlier and more conventional notions of wisdom.

In the earlier scriptures of the Pali Canon, wisdom (*pañña*, which later took the Sanskrit form *prajña* in the Mahayana) was identified with understanding the non-substantiality of the self. The self was perceived as a congruence of functions, and these, in turn, as a series of events or units of experience, known as *dharmas*. As scholastic Buddhism developed, the nature of these dharmas became a primary focus of attention. Understanding the flux of dharmas, from which the illusion of self arose, became a matter of importance and some fascination. Dharmas were conceptualized, listed, typed, and classified. Differing views on their nature and interaction engendered different schools of thought. Wisdom became, in short, a rational and analytic exercise, comprising enumerations, categories, and conjecture. The debates threatened to go on endlessly, when, from the wings, a new wisdom moved onto the scene.

Because she pointed to a reality that eludes classifications, this wisdom, *prajña*, was called *paramita*, which means "gone beyond" or to the "other side," as well as "perfection."

To those who were dryly and doggedly analyzing the dharmas, she offered not theories, but paradoxes. "Countless beings do I lead to nirvana and yet there are none who are led to nirvana." "The bodhisattva will go forth—but he will not go forth to anywhere." "In the Buddha's teachings he trains, [but] no training is this training and no one is trained." "In his jubilation he transforms all dharmas, but none are transformed, for dharmas are illusory."[1]

No formula captured her insight, but through the paradoxes shone a light offering release from the self-adhesive nature of human logic. The self is non-substantial, and so are its concepts, including the very dharmas into which the self was analyzed. They are as empty of "own being" as the self. Thus does Perfection of Wisdom return to the Buddha's quintessential doctrine, the radical interdependence, or interbeing, of all things.

In the text it is Sariputra, traditionally revered as the Buddha's most learned disciple, who represents the scholastic mentality. Weighted with logic and literalness, he struggles with the apparent contradictions of the new wisdom and asks questions that are answered by the Buddha and Subhuti, a follower who is now raised up as an example of one who sees into the interdependently co-arising nature of things. The paradoxes, as Sariputra learns, leave the observing ego with no safe place to stand, knocking away the concepts that perpetuate it.

This wisdom, then, is not the kind one can think oneself into. It is a way of seeing. Without it, the very practice of virtue and meditation can be a prop for ego, to which we cling in pride or desperation. With it, the world itself is altered—not suppressed or rejected, but transfigured.

CLEAR LIGHT, DEEP SPACE

> The Buddhas in the world-systems in the ten directions
>
> bring to mind this perfection of wisdom as their mother.
>
> The Saviors of the world who were in the past, and also are
> now in the ten directions,
>
> Have issued from her, and so will the future ones be.
>
> She is the one who shows this world [for what it is],
>
> she is the genetrix, the mother of all the Buddhas.[2]

The mother, like the wisdom she offers, is elusive. She is barely personalized in the sutra; no stories are attached to her, no direct speech is accorded her, no physical descriptions of her are offered. None of the gestures, colors, or adornments that will figure in the images made of her centuries later are presented. The dozen or so epithets for her in the sutra appear mostly in passing, as if self-explanatory—"Prajnaparamita, the mother," "Mother of the Tathagatas," "Mother of the Sugatas," "Mother of the bodhisattvas," "instructress of the Tathagatas in this world," "genetrix and nurse of the six perfections."

The feminine character of this wisdom is conveyed in many analogies. In their eagerness to learn and experience enlightenment, bodhisattvas are likened to "a pregnant woman, all astir with pains, whose time has come for her to give birth." In their devotion to the welfare of other beings, they are "like a mother, ministering to her only child." In their constant pondering of this wisdom, they are like a man who had made a date with an attractive woman. "And if now that woman were held back by someone else and could not leave her house, what do you think, Subhuti," asks the Buddha, "with what would that man's preoccupations be connected?" "With the woman, of course," Subhuti answers, "he thinks about her coming, about the things they will do together, and about the joy, fun, and delight he will have with her." "Just as preoccupied as such a man," says the Lord, "is the bodhisattva with thoughts of the Perfection of Wisdom."[3]

And when the bodhisattva meets her, what qualities does he find in her? He finds light, emptiness, space, and a world-confronting gaze that is both clinical and compassionate. "The Perfection of Wisdom gives light, O Lord. I pay homage to the Perfection of Wisdom!" cries Sariputra, after listening to Subhuti and the Buddha. "She is a source of light, and from everyone in the triple world she removes darkness. . . . She brings light to the blind, she brings light so that all fear and distress may be forsaken. She has gained the five eyes, and she shows the path to all beings. She herself is an organ of vision."[4]

As light and insight, she reveals that all dharmas are void, signless, and wishless, not-produced, not-stopped, and non-existent. By the same token, Perfect Wisdom herself is empty (sunya). She is "not a real thing." Like dharmas, Buddhas, and bodhisattvas, she offers "no basis for apprehension." The sutra acknowledges that this is fearful to contemplate, that this teaching is "alarming" and "terrifying." Those who are "not frightened on hearing the Mother's deep tenets," who are "not cowed, paralyzed, or stupefied," "who do not despair, turn away, or become dejected," reveal their potential for full Buddhahood.[5]

While Perfection of Wisdom reveals sunyata, the void, in all its awesomeness, she seems to recognize the terror it can initially induce, for she also offers comfort. "In her we find defense and protection." "She offers the safety of the wings of enlightenment."

"She helps with the four grounds of self-confidence."[6] The reassurance she gives is symbolized in the *abhaya mudra* of her raised right hand, the fear-not gesture that we encounter in some later Tantric images of her.

Her compassion is not seen as a cradling, cuddling, or clasping to the bosom. Rather it inheres in her very seeing and is implicit in her clear-eyed vision of the world's suffering. The many eyes, to which Sariputra referred in connection with her illuminating insight, become symbolic of this compassion. When she assumes the form of Tara, these eyes, set in her forehead, hands, and feet, express her caring. It is not surprising that metaphors of sheltering and enclosing are relatively rare for the Perfection of Wisdom. Since, as the bodhisattva is repeatedly reminded, there is no ground to stand on, the predominant movement is to imagine her in space, in boundless immensity.

In *akasa*, the infinite expanse of space, the notions of light and void conjoin. In this sutra lies the metaphor par excellence for the Perfection of Wisdom. Like space, she is endless (*ananta*). Like space, she is immeasurable, incalculable, and insubstantial; like space, she cannot be increased, decreased, or confined in categories. Like sheer space, she can terrify, but the bodhisattvas must plunge right into it, unafraid and ready to delight. If they can trust her, they become "like a bird that on its wings courses in the air. It neither falls to the ground, nor does it stand anywhere on any support. It dwells in space, just as in the air, without being either supported or settled therein."

This space, into which the bodhisattva ventures, is not the old realm of the sky gods, traditionally accorded to the male in the mythic dualities of sky father/earth mother. Attributes of the sky father featured the sovereign heights of his heavens, his astronomic regularity and law, the power of his thunderous downpours. No such references are made to the Mother of the Buddhas, no allusions to the majesty, order, or power of heavenly phenomena. The one attribute she shares with him is that of all-seeing. Furthermore, she is not set in opposition to the recumbent earth; on the contrary, she is, on occasion, metaphorically equated with it as the ground of being. "As many trees, fruits, flowers as there are have all come out of the earth . . . [so have] the Buddha's offspring and the gods and the dharmas issued from Perfect Wisdom." This wisdom is also linked with Earth by the act ascribed to the Buddha during his enlightenment vigil, in which he called her to witness. He reached down and touched her, affirming his right to attain freedom.

The measureless space of the Perfection of Wisdom extends not only outward and up, but also inward and down. It is deep space. "Deep is the Perfection of Wisdom," says Subhuti. And the Lord answers, "Yes, with a depth like that of space."

THE PREGNANT ZERO

A rich and startling dimension is added to the Perfection of Wisdom when we learn how terms that describe her played a role in the development of mathematics. To be specific, she influenced the emergence of zero. The early numerical system developed by the Babylonians was hampered by having no such concept or symbol. It was Indian mathematicians in the early centuries CE who evolved the decimal system and the crucially important notion of zero. All of this, transmitted to the West by Arab traders, became the basis for European numbering and computation.

Cultural historian Ananda K. Coomaraswamy has pointed out that in India, previous to numerical notations, verbal symbols were used technically. For the concept of zero, in particular, a variety of terms was employed, and these technical verbal symbols derived from Indian metaphysics. Now, several of these words for zero, such as sunya, akasa, and ananta, served as chief attributes assigned to the Perfection of Wisdom, Mother of all Buddhas.

The apparent opposition between some of the terms used for zero—for example, *purna* (full), along with sunya (empty)—is interpreted by Coomaraswamy to indicate that "to the Indian mind all numbers are virtually or potentially present in that which is without number . . . (or) that zero is to number as possibility is to actuality." He further reflects that the use of ananta (endless) implies an identification of zero with infinity—"the beginning of all series being thus the same as their end." Akasa represents "primarily not a concept of physical space, but of a purely principal space without dimension, although the matrix of dimension."[7]

This zero space becomes the still center of the turning world. *Kha* and *nabha*, two other terms for zero used technically by mathematicians, originally meant the hole in the hub of a wheel through which the axle runs. For the wheel to revolve, the center must be empty. Hence, probably, the sign for zero. It is the circle in which end and beginning merge. It is also a sexual sign for the female, linking the feminine and the void, as does the Perfection of Wisdom. Around the emptiness, sunyata, she represents, the Wheel of the Dharma turns. That void is, as D. T. Suzuki said, "not an abstraction but an experience, or a deed enacted where there is neither space nor time."[8]

Note the Mother's attitude vis-a-vis this world. The liberation offered by the Perfection of Wisdom is not attained by
turning away from samsara. "Those who are certain that they
have got safely out of this world are unfit for full enlightenment," says the sutra. The light that she bestows does not dazzle,
eclipse, or blind one to mundane phenomena and the traffic
of beings; but, clear and cool, it illumines the world "as it is."
The capacity to see reality *as it is (yathabutham)*, fully accepting the multiplicities and particularities of things, is repeatedly
stressed as a gift of the Mother of All Buddhas. While the world
is often presented in the text as dream, illusion, and magic
show, one does not shun it, for there is nothing that is more
real or in whose pursuit the bodhisattva would lift his gaze
from things-as-they-are.

The Mother of the Buddhas, therefore, does not call the
bodhisattvas beyond this world to final nirvana. She retains
them on this side of reality for the sake of all beings. "In this
dwelling of Perfect Wisdom . . . you shall become a savior of
the helpless, a defender of the defenseless . . . a light to the
blind, and you shall guide to the path those who have lost it,
and you shall become a support to those who are without
support." In such passages as these, the bodhisattva path is
described, for the first time, as a summons to all persons. The
skill in means (*upaya*) by which the bodhisattva responds
and acts within the realm of contingency and need is seen as
essential to his enlightenment. Upaya, the readiness to reach
out and improvise, is the other face of wisdom. Together
they constitute the ground for ethical action and delight—
revalorizing samsara while assigning no fixed reality to its
varied manifestations.

Such is the wisdom of the Mother of all Buddhas, empty of preconception, the pregnant point of potential action, beholding the teeming world with a vision that transfigures. When she is later portrayed as Green Tara, her gestures will recall this active, compassionate aspect; the right arm is outstretched to help, and the right leg, no longer tucked up in the aloof serenity of the lotus posture, extends downward, ready to step into the world.

NEITHER TEMPTRESS NOR TRAP

To appreciate the distinctiveness of the Perfection of Wisdom, we must see how her symbolization as wisdom, light, and space runs counter to the feminine archetype prevailing in Hindu culture. There we find a worldview rooted in polarities between earth and sky, nature and consciousness, matter and mind.

The aboriginal, pre-Aryan culture centered around worship of a fertility goddess. Like other neolithic societies, it worshipped the productivity of nature (seen as female because of its birthing capacity), while recognizing its remorseless vegetative cycle of growth and death. The goddess of the Indus Valley and Dravidian culture was driven underground by the invading Aryans and their chariot-driving warrior sky-gods. Centuries later she resurfaced, clothed in respectability, in the Samkhya philosophy, which had a profound and formative effect on subsequent Indian thought. Samkhya reestablished her in the form of the eternally evolving and fecund *prakrti*, the nature principle. She is dynamic and unconscious, in contrast to *purusa*, the conscious spirit. The individual soul is entrapped in prakrti's turbulent world of change and materiality, and it is only in extricating from her that transcendence and release can be won.

The ancient matriarchal element also reasserted itself in the later development of the Devi and her cult. Represented variously as Durga and Kali and other female forms, she is essentially the one and original Devi, the goddess. Whether adorned with peacock feathers or garlanded with skulls, she is the ceaselessly active one, prakrti, maya, shakti. She is the restlessness of primal matter, the fecund and cruel mother. As the creative power of the male gods, from whom she issues, she complements their pure, passive intelligence.

The goddess is both indulgent and terrible. Ambivalent feelings about the mother figure she symbolizes are reflected in the dual status of women in traditional Hindu society. As a sexual partner, the woman often tends to be presented as a dangerous and enfeebling seductress, a semen-stealer. But as a mother—the mother of a son, that is—she is revered and accorded prerogatives denied her as a person. Although birthing a son elevates her status, she is expected to remain ever subservient to him. Consequently, the indulgence that a mother lavishes on her son is not unmixed; as anthropologist Richard Lannoy puts it, "with her feeling of maternal love co-exist feelings of envy and retaliation."[9] Lannoy, studying this phenomenon, links it with the prevalence of "the terrible mother" in Hindu myth and finds its imagery expressive of both dependence and aggression.

In any event, there are philosophic grounds for this image of the feminine in the Hindu world. Differing apprehensions of reality lie at the root of the contrast between the Devi and the Perfection of Wisdom. A metaphysical dichotomy between consciousness and nature leads to a vision of spirit as struggling to be free from the toils of matter. Matter comes to be seen as polluting and binding, her fertile nature as arbitrary, lavish, cruel.

Jungian psychologist James Hillman shows that a love-hate relationship with matter is endemic in the Great Mother complex and is evident today in contemporary values. When the archetypal mother is linked with the earthly in opposition to the psyche, a dual response is elicited from the son or spirit: rebellion and possession. Either the spirit rebels by subjugating matter, be it by mortification of the flesh or destruction of the land, or it seeks to seduce and possess the mother by accumulating and consuming her goods and resources. Either way, matter (*mater*) exerts her power and fascination.

The Mother of All Buddhas escapes this role and presents a completely different feminine archetype. The doctrine of interdependent co-arising permits no polarization of consciousness and nature. Matter, seen as co-emergent with mind, is neither temptress nor trap. Faith in this wisdom mother is very different, therefore, from devotion accorded to the Devi. The Perfection of Wisdom is not a mother to be placated and cajoled. Faith in her is not a seeking of favors, but a letting go, a falling into emptiness. It is the release of one's clutching onto dharmas and concepts, a venturing outward, a leaning into space. Seeing through the fiction of a separate self, one passes through the zero point. Because such a zero experience is a kind of birth, generative of new worlds, it is fitting that she who leads us through it is seen as genetrix and mother.

Centuries later, in a profusion of graphic imagery, the Perfection of Wisdom became the prototype of all the female figures featured in Buddhist Tantric interplay. With serene aplomb she copulates with upaya, skillful means. Her other face, compassionate action, has become her male consort.

Scholars and art lovers have wondered and debated why, in these Buddhist figures, the sexual roles are reversed from the Hindu brand of Tantrism. There in connubial embrace, it is Shiva who is the sublimely passive partner, while his consort, Shakti, represents dynamism. We now understand why the Perfection of Wisdom cannot, without misrepresentation, be equated with Shakti, or even Shiva, for that matter. The Buddhist *yab-yum* (male-female embrace) embodies a different vision altogether.

The fundamental difference is ontological: Perfection of Wisdom is empty, devoid of independent being, whereas Shiva (as wisdom) is the ultimate essence with which, by aid of Shakti, the adept would merge. In the Hindu pair, maya (material manifestation) is subsumed into *moksha* (spirit and release). In contrast to this, the Tantric symbolism of Buddhism represents not a canceling or absorption of one pole, but the continual interplay of both. These poles are not moksha and maya or pure consciousness over or against energy/matter, but rather two kinds of consciousness/energy. In the embrace of prajña and upaya, wisdom and skillful means, life's dialectic modes of vision and action are held in balance, being complementary and mutually essential. That numinous copulation reflects the interdependent co-arising of all things.

Appearing both as luminous space and compassionate caller of bodhisattvas, Prajnaparamita, the Mother of All Buddhas, conveys a transforming vision of the world. In her, and through her, the central insight of the Buddha is rediscovered and reaffirmed; and that is why the scriptures that honor her are known as the Second Turning of the Wheel of the Dharma.

PART THREE

Food for the Heart

TEN

OPENINGS

What was said to the rose that made it open
was said to me here in my chest.

—JALALUDDIN RUMI

Some experiences seem to change the shape of who we are and leave us reconfigured—with gateways where there had been walls, and closet doors leading to wild woodlands and the sea. Whether suddenly complete or slowly unfolding, these experiences are always a gift—whole, sufficient, and free of doubt. Here are two that grace my life ongoingly.

THE MAPLE TREE

Approaching the main house on my grandfather's farm, you would see a maple tree, standing alone beside the road, tall and graceful. She did not live in the company of her own kind, as the fruit trees did; she—and this tree was definitely a *she* for me—seemed more self-reliant and self-contained. I knew her for eight summers, from the age of nine through the summer I was sixteen.

The maple opened out a good distance from the ground, so I had to leap and scramble to hoist myself up. Straddling the lowest, waist-thick branch and slowly pulling myself upright, I entered a solitude that was more than my own. It was a protected solitude, like the woods near the north pasture, but different, because here one single living being was holding me. My hands still remember the feel of her: the texture of the gray bark, the way it rippled in folds near the joints, its dusting of powder. As I climbed up into her murmuring canopy, my heart quickened—from fear of falling and from awe. Caution felt like reverence.

Here in the maple I didn't play games, the way I did in the wide old apple tree that my older brother Harty had rigged with platforms. There I played practically every day, not with Harty, who returned to his own pursuits, but with my little brother John. The scarred, angular old apple became a schooner, a submarine, a spaceship, cliffs and ledges for our assaults on Everest, jungle encampments in the heart of Africa, bombers and fighter planes dodging Hitler's anti-aircraft batteries. From a high branch hung a swing whose ropes could be drawn up and grabbed from within the tree. And each adventure required, at some point, that heart-stopping leap from the heights, a timeless free fall before the ropes caught and the board swung you out over the speeding ground.

The maple tree did not invite pretending games. I only went there alone. It was a place to be quiet, a place to disappear into a kind of shared presence: the being that was tree and me, with the light coming through. The light is what I remember most of all. High and wide around me, it shaped a luminous, breathing bowl. It danced through the leaves, glowing them green and gold, it stroked the limbs with flickering shadows. When I stayed very quiet, the play of light seemed to go right through my body, and my own breath was part of the maple's murmuring.

Being there was sufficient. I didn't think about my life. I didn't talk to the maple about the cares and fears I had begun to carry. The maple took me into a vast, lit stillness beyond all that. She let me glimpse a wild serenity at the heart of my world.

The maple, my cloister, was not remote; she stood diagonally in front of the house beside the road that linked us to town. She held her stillness and mystery right in the middle of things. Traffic on our farm road passed almost under her branches, although with gas rationing, the cars and trucks and tractors were few those years, even after the road was paved in 1943. After the war, when the traffic got heavier and faster, the road was widened, and the maple disappeared. I had gone by then, but the maple tree is still alive in me.

THE MILKY WAY

In graduate school, in my forties, I took a trip to India on my own. Our family had moved to a big old inner-city house and exchanged our nuclear family pattern for cooperative living with an equal number of assorted non-Macys. This was engrossing for us all and further liberated me into my doctoral studies.

I had been away from India for a decade, and I returned eager for immediacy of contact with ancient India. I was free this time from concerns for the health and whereabouts of the three children, which I knew well from our years living there as a family. Eager to taste the tang of adventure, the three months I had taken for the journey were wonderfully rewarding for me. Central was my exploration into the most ancient art in

India, *aniconic* imagery, in which, in the early four centuries after the Buddha lived, he was not shown as a human figure but was symbolized by other life forms. My favorite depicted the Buddha as a tree, representing his enlightenment.

I journeyed by train, bus, and cart to the most ancient stupas, where the gates and railings bore carvings depicting scenes of those never-to-be-forgotten days when the Buddha was alive. In these scenes, an elephant represents the Buddha's birth, the tree his awakening, the wheel his teaching, and the stupa his death.

I was especially drawn to the image of the tree. Tree worship had been India's primordial religious practice, and it delighted me that as the Buddhist movement emerged, it did not set itself against the adoration of nature. This was all the more striking to me, recalling how Jahweh had told his people to cut down the sacred groves when they entered Canaan, just as the Vatican, in a later era, ordered its emissaries to fell the ancient oak groves in extending its power over Britain. Yet here in India, it was the opposite, and this was part of my fascination with this tree imagery.

My other exploration during those three months was much newer. It had begun twenty years before, when a growing leader of India's Untouchables, the brilliant Ambedkar, decided to break with Gandhi and leave Hinduism, because it could not be separated from the caste system. In 1956, he and three hundred thousand of his followers had converted to Buddhism in an historic ceremony in Nagpur. They had been Dalits, meaning "the broken ones," and in the caste system, they were the very lowest rung, marked by the stamp of "Untouchable," subject to horrific treatment and historically excluded from any religious

activity. I fell in love with these new Buddhists and the serious-
ness with which they took the Buddha's dharma. Visiting their
shrines in the city slums and traveling to their new institutions
of learning in Aurangabad, I talked late at night with their pro-
fessors in their homes. As unexpected friendships flowered, I
felt the plenitude and grace in the Buddhdharma itself.

One of these flowerings was a relationship with a Gandh-
ian leper colony in the heart of India. As my three months drew
to a close, I had a distinct feeling the trip would be incomplete
unless I returned to say goodbye to my friends there. Before my
departure, with a day to spare before my flight home, I headed
off to see my friends who ran the place, having no idea the
night would bring me an experience that would outlast everything else.

I loved each chance I got to sleep outside. After dinner my
friends set up a rope-strung *charpoi* for me to sleep on near
their veranda. As I finally relaxed my body's full weight on the
thin mattress over the rope webbing, my mind traveled back
over the day—the train changes to get me to Wardha Junction,
the bicycle rickshaw three miles to Dattapur, arriving in time
to greet my friends and walk with them through the colony.
Familiar sights and new ones, my gladness in the faces. The flute
music I recognized, my delight in seeing its turbaned player,
and the old question that came to mind: *With the growing
numbness of leprosy, won't his flute playing wear out his fingers
more quickly?* Adrift in these memories, I soon fell asleep under
a heaven full of stars.

Sometime near midnight or early morning I awoke. Opening my eyes, my gaze fell straight into the middle of the stars. I
seemed at first to be looking down into them. Tipped to the south

was the Milky Way, with skeins and billows of light clouds strewn among its stars and dark pockets where my gaze could drown. It was a living presence, in which I awoke to the sense of being welcomed, a sense of homecoming as sweet as tears.

"*My heart has been washed*" were the words that came out of me. All self-criticism and the crossness of self-betterment and the ambition of self-schooling was washed away, leaving me a plain, pure, sufficient part of my world.

My gaze into the sky stirred a nearly out-of-reach recognition of something terribly important I had almost forgotten, losing it again and again my whole life. I could not understand or make up for the continual forgetting, all I could do was rest in the current of love being directed into my chest. It came from a particular place in the Milky Way, just to the right of its zenith above me. I felt it speaking to me, giving utterance to a central fact, common to both of us—self and universe—a mutual, endless belonging. Totally, unconditionally, with a love too deep to celebrate—a shared secret, a common trust, a reciprocal necessity, one mind.

An incompletely remembered, almost hackneyed phrase from Kant echoed in my head, "Two things . . . *something* . . . *something* . . . the starry heavens above and the moral law within."* What had been a cliché became a shuddering insight when I saw it as an equation or equivalency. The "moral law within" was none other than the depthless wonder of the skies into which my gaze plummeted, and to which I belonged.

I lay there in such quiet joy, pulling the blanket up under my chin, closing my eyes only to open them again into that encounter, that statement—accepting the wonder of it and this self of mine, too.

The sun was already warm on my face when I felt my friend Deepak tapping my arm. "Joanna, we found a car for you to Wardha Junction. You can get a connection to your airport bus from there."

---

*Full quote: "Two things fill the mind with ever new and increasing admiration and awe, the oftener and more steadily we reflect on them: the starry heavens above me and the moral law within me. I do not seek or conjecture either of them as if they were veiled obscurities or extravagances beyond the horizon of my vision; I see them before me and connect them immediately with the consciousness of my existence." Immanuel Kant, *Critique of Practical Reason*, rev. ed., trans. and ed. Mary Gregor (Cambridge: Cambridge University Press, 2015), original 1788.

ELEVEN

THE GREENING
OF THE SELF

May we turn inwards and stumble upon our true roots
in the intertwining biology of this exquisite planet.
May nourishment and power pulse through these roots,
and fierce determination to continue the billion-year dance.

—JOHN SEED

Something important is happening in our world that gets drowned out by all the alarming information vying for our attention. I consider it the most fascinating and hopeful development of our time, and it is one of the reasons I am so glad to be alive today. It has to do with our notion of the self.

The self is a metaphoric construct for our identity and agency, the hypothetical piece of turf on which we construct our strategies for survival, the notion around which we focus our instincts for self-preservation, our needs for self-approval, and the boundaries of our self-interest. Something is shifting here. The conventional notion of the self with which we have been raised and to which we have been conditioned by five centuries of hyper-individualism is being undermined. What Alan Watts called "the skin-encapsulated ego" and Gregory Bateson referred to as "the epistemological error of Occidental civilization" is cracking open from its constricting shell. It is being replaced by wider constructs of identity and self-interest—by what philosopher Arne Naess termed the "ecological self," coextensive with other beings and the life of our planet. It is what I like to call "the greening of the self."

BODHISATTVAS IN RUBBER BOATS

In a lecture on a college campus some decades back, I gave examples of activities being undertaken in defense of life on Earth—actions in which people risk their comfort and even their lives to protect other species. In the Chipko tree-hugging movement in northern India, for example, villagers were protecting their remaining forests from ax and bulldozer by interposing their bodies. On the open seas in small zodiac rafts, Greenpeace activists were intervening to protect marine mammals from slaughter. After that talk, I received a letter from a student I'll call Michael. He wrote:

> I think of the tree-huggers hugging my trunk, blocking the chain saws with their bodies. I feel their fingers digging into my bark to stop the steel and let me breathe. I hear the bodhisattvas in their rubber boats as they put themselves between the harpoons and me, so I can escape to the depths of the sea. I give thanks for your life and mine, and for life itself. I give thanks for realizing that I too have the powers of the tree-huggers and the bodhisattvas.

What is striking about Michael's words is the shift in identification. Michael was able to extend his sense of self to encompass the self of a tree and of a whale. Tree and whale were no longer remote, separate, marketable objects "out there"; they were intrinsic to his own life. Through the power of his caring, his experience of self was expanded far beyond that skin-encapsulated ego. I quote Michael's words not because they were unusual, but to the contrary, because they expressed a desire and a capacity that was being released from the prison cell of old constructs of self. This desire and capacity are arising in more and more people today, out of deep concern for what is happening to our world and as they act on its behalf.

Among those who are shedding these old constructs of self, like old skin or a confining shell, is John Seed, founder of the Rainforest Information Centre in Australia. One day in 1985 we were walking through the rainforest in New South Wales, near his office in a vine-covered bus, and I asked him, "You talk about the struggle against the lumber companies and politicians to save the remaining rainforests. How do you deal with the despair?"

He replied, "I try to remember that it's not me, John Seed, trying to protect the rainforest. Rather, I am part of the rainforest protecting itself. I am the part that has recently emerged into human thinking." This is what I mean by the greening of the self. It involves a combining of the mystical with the pragmatic, transcending separateness, alienation, and fragmentation. It is a shift that Seed himself calls "a spiritual change," generating a sense of profound interconnectedness with all life.

This is hardly new to our species. In the past, poets and mystics have spoken and written about these ideas and experiences, but not people on the barricades, agitating for change. The sense of an encompassing self, a deep identity with the wider reaches of life, has now become a motivation for action.

It is a source of courage that helps us stand up to the powers that are still, through the force of inertia, engaged in the destruction of our world. This expanded sense of self leads to sustained and resilient action on behalf of life.

When you look at what is happening to our world, it has become clear that unless you have some roots in a spiritual practice that holds life sacred and encourages communion with your fellow beings, facing the enormous challenges ahead becomes nearly impossible.

Robert Bellah's classic book *Habits of the Heart*, published in 1985, was not a place where you would read about the greening of the self. But it is where you could read about *why* there has to be a greening of the self, because it described the cramp that our society had gotten itself into. Bellah pointed out that the individualism embodied in and inflamed by the industrial growth society is accelerating. It not only causes alienation and fragmentation in our society but is also endangering our survival. Bellah calls for a *moral ecology*. "We have to treat others as part of who we are," he says, "rather than as a 'them' with whom we are in constant competition."[1]

To Robert Bellah, I respond, "It is happening." It is happening, I believe, because of three converging developments. First, the conventional small self, or ego-self, is being psychologically and spiritually challenged by confrontation with our feelings of grief as we see what's happening to our world. The second force working to dismantle the ego-self is a way of seeing that has arisen out of science. From living systems theory and systems cybernetics has emerged a process view of the self as inseparable from the web of relationships that sustain it. The third force is the resurgence in our time of nondualistic spiritualities. Here

I write from my own experience with Buddhist thought and practice, but I see it happening in other faith traditions as well, such as the Jewish Renewal Movement, Creation Spirituality in Christianity, and Sufism in Islam, as well as in the appreciation being given to the teachings of indigenous cultures. For some time I've been thinking how these developments are impinging on the self in ways that are helping it to break out of its old boundaries and definitions.

CRACKED OPEN BY GRIEF

The move to a wider, ecological sense of self is, in large part, a function of the dangers that threaten to overwhelm us. Given news reports pointing to the progressive destruction of our biosphere, awareness grows that the world as we know it may come to an end. Why do I claim that this erodes the old sense of self? Because once we stop denying the crises of our time and let ourselves experience the depth of our own responses to the suffering of our world—whether it is the burning of the Amazon rainforest or the homeless in our own cities—the grief or anger or fear we experience cannot be reduced to concerns for our own skin. When we mourn the destruction of our bio- sphere, it is categorically distinct from grief at the prospect of our own personal death.

Planetary anguish lifts us onto another systemic level, where we open to larger dimensions of experience. It enables us to recognize our profound interconnectedness with all beings. Don't apologize if you cry for the burning of the Amazon or the Appalachian Mountains blasted open for strip mining! The sorrow and rage you feel is a measure of your humanity and your evolutionary maturity. As your heart breaks open, there will be room for the world to heal. That is what is happening as we see people honestly confronting the sorrows of our time. And it is an adaptive, necessary response.

The crisis that threatens our planet, whether seen in its military, ecological, or social aspect, derives from a dysfunctional and pathological notion of the self. It stems from a mistake about our place in the order of things. It is the delusion that the self is so separate and fragile that we must delineate and defend its boundaries; that it is so small and so needy that we must endlessly acquire and endlessly consume; and that, as individuals, corporations, nation-states, or a species, we can be immune to what we do to other beings.

The urge to move beyond such a constricted view of self is not new, of course. Humans from all times have felt the imperative to extend their self-interest to embrace the whole. What is notable in our current situation is that this extension of identity comes not through a desire to be good or altruistic, but simply to be more fully present to our world, however hard that may be. And that is why this shift in the sense of self is credible to people.

CYBERNETICS OF THE SELF

Twentieth-century science undermined the notion of a self that is distinct from the world it observes and acts upon. Einstein showed that the self's perceptions are determined by its position in relation to other phenomena. And Werner Heisenberg, in his uncertainty principle, demonstrated that its perceptions are altered by the very act of observation.

Systems science goes further in challenging old assumptions about a separate, continuous self, by showing that there is no logical or scientific basis for construing one part of the experienced world as "me" and the rest as "other." As open, self-organizing systems, our very breathing, acting, and thinking arise in interaction with our shared world through the currents of matter, energy, and information that move through us. In the web of relationships that sustain these activities, there is no line of demarcation between self and other. There is no categorical "I" set over against a categorical "you" or "it."

One of the clearest expositions of this is found in the writings of Gregory Bateson, who says that the process that decides and acts cannot be neatly identified with the isolated subjectivity of the individual or located within the confines of the skin. He contends that "the total self-corrective unit that processes information is a system whose boundaries may not coincide with the boundaries either of the body or what is popularly called 'self' or 'consciousness.'" He goes on to say, "The self as ordinarily understood is only a small part of a much larger trial-and-error system which does the thinking, acting, and deciding."[2]

Bateson offers two helpful examples. One is a woodcutter in the process of felling a tree. His hands grip the handle of the ax, there is the head of the ax, the trunk of the tree. *Whump!* he makes a cut, and then *whump!* another cut. What is felling the tree? Is it not the information flow or feedback circuit that is guiding the process? It is a whole loop that can be blocked at any point from the eye of the woodcutter, to the hand, to the ax, to the cut in the tree. That self-correcting unit, says Bateson, is what is chopping down the tree.

In another illustration, a blind person with a cane is walking along the sidewalk. *Tap, tap,* whoops, there's a fire hydrant,
there's the curb. Now who actually is steering the process of
walking? What is doing the perceiving and deciding? The self-
corrective feedback circuit includes the arm, the hand, the cane,
the curb, and the ear. At that moment, that is the self that is
walking. Bateson points out that our usual notion of the self is
a false reification of an improperly delimited part of a much
larger field of interlocking processes. And he goes on to maintain that "this false reification of the self is basic to the planetary
ecological crisis in which we find ourselves. We have imagined
that the unit of survival is the separate individual or a separate
species, whereas in reality, through the history of evolution it is
the individual plus the environment, the species plus the environment, for they are essentially symbiotic."[3]

As Bateson explained, our self-reflexive, purposive consciousness illuminates but a small arc in the currents and loops of
knowing that interweave us. It is just as plausible to conceive
of mind as coexistent with these larger circuits, with the entire
"pattern that connects."

SPIRITUAL BREAKTHROUGHS

The third factor that has helped dismantle the conventional
notion of the self is the resurgence of nondualistic spiritualities. This trend can be found in all faith traditions. I have found
Buddhism to be distinctive for the clarity and sophistication it
brings to understanding the dynamics of the self. In much the
same way as systems theory does, Buddhism undermines the
dichotomy between self and other and rejects the concept of a

continuous, self-existent entity. It then goes further in showing the pathogenic character of any reifications of the self. It goes further still in offering methods for transcending these limits and healing the suffering they cause.

Over the eons, in every religion, we have wondered: *What do we do with the self*—this clamorous "I," or ego, always wanting attention, always wanting its goodies? Should we crucify, sacrifice, and mortify it? Or should we affirm, improve, and ennoble it?

The Buddhist path leads us to realize that all we need to do with the self is see through it. It's just a convention—a convenient convention, to be sure, but with no greater reality than that. When you take it too seriously, when you suppose that it is something enduring that you have to defend and promote, it becomes the foundation of delusion, the origins of our attachments and aversions.

Our pain for the world, when felt without fear, reveals our true nature as one with the entirety of life. The being who knows that is the bodhisattva. Each of us can recognize and act from our inter-existence with all beings. When we turn our eyes away from that homeless figure, are we indifferent, or is the pain of seeing them too great? Do not be deceived by the apparent indifference of those around you. What looks like apathy may be reluctance to activate the anguish already felt. But the Buddhist hero with the boundless heart knows that if you're afraid to get close to the pain of our world, you'll be distanced from its joy as well.

One thing I love about the ecological self is that it makes moral exhortation irrelevant. Sermonizing can be both tedious and ineffective. This is pointed out by Arne Naess, the

Norwegian philosopher who coined the terms *deep ecology* and *ecological self.*

Naess explains that we change the way we experience our self through an ever-widening process of identification. Borrowing from the Hindu tradition, he calls this process *self-realization*—a progression "where the self to be realized extends further and further beyond the separate ego and includes more and more of the phenomenal world." And he goes on to say, "Unfortunately, the extensive moralizing within the ecological movement has given the public the false impression that they are being asked to make a sacrifice—to show more responsibility, more concern, and a nicer moral standard. But all of that would flow naturally and easily if the self were widened and deepened so that the protection of nature was felt and perceived as protection of our very selves."[4]

The emergence of the ecological self at this point in our history is required precisely *because* moral exhortation does not work. Sermons seldom hinder us from following our self-interest as we conceive it.

The obvious choice, then, is to extend our notions of self-interest. For example, it would not occur to you to saw off your leg because your leg is part of your body. Well, so are the trees in the Amazon rainforest. They're our external lungs. We are beginning to realize that the world is our body.

The ecological self, like any notion of selfhood, is a metaphoric construct, useful for what it allows us to perceive and how it helps us to behave. It is dynamic and situational, a perspective we can choose to adopt according to context and need. We can choose to identify at different moments with different dimensions or aspects of our systemically interrelated existence—be they dying rivers or stranded refugees or the planet itself. In so doing, the extension of self brings wider resources into awareness. With these realizations comes a sense of resilience. From the wider web that cradles our life, we can invite resources like courage, endurance, and ingenuity to flow through us.

By expanding our self-interest to include other beings in the body of Earth, the ecological self also widens our window on time. It enlarges our temporal context, freeing us from identifying our goals and rewards solely in terms of our present lifetime. The life pouring through us, pumping our heart and breathing through our lungs, did not begin at our birth or conception. Like every particle and atom of our bodies, it goes back through time to the first galaxies and stars.

Thus, the greening of the self helps us to reinhabit time and own our story as life on Earth. We were present from the start—in the rains that streamed down on this still-molten planet and in the primordial seas. In our mother's womb we remembered that journey, growing vestigial gills and tail and fins. Beneath the outer layers of our neocortex and what we learned in school, that story is in us—the story of a kinship with all life, which brings strengths beyond what we can imagine. When we claim this story as our own, a gladness comes, and that deep familiarity will guide us.

TWELVE

FAITH, POWER, AND
DEEP ECOLOGY

And who will join this standing up?
And the ones who stood without sweet company
will sing and sing
back into the mountains and
even under the sea.

—JUNE JORDAN

These words take me back to a morning in Great Britain. In the early autumn of 1986, I was standing for an hour in the sweet, gentle English drizzle. Some thirty men and women, three holding toddlers, were standing with me in a large meadow. Gathered there at the close of a workshop on deep ecology, our band included activists from all over the United Kingdom—social workers, civil servants, artisans, teachers, homemakers—drawn together by a common concern for the fate of our world. At the center of our wide circle rose two ancient, sacred standing stones.

In the presence of the standing stones, thousands of years old, we found ourselves in two dimensions of time simultaneously. One was vast and immeasurable. As we reached back to the ancient Earth wisdom of the culture that erected the stones, we sensed the long, long journey of life unfolding on this planet. At the same time, we were acutely aware of our own historical moment when forces unleashed by our culture were already threatening to destroy our world.

We were people of varied religious traditions—or none—yet, despite our differing backgrounds, the prayers and affirmations spontaneously spoken in that circle expressed a common faith and fueled a common hope. They conveyed a shared commitment to engage in actions and changes in lifestyle on behalf of our Earth and its beings. The words expressed a deep connection to Earth, extending beyond feeling sorry for the planet or scared for ourselves. They were an affirmation of faithful relationship that is spiritually as well as physically sustaining, a relationship that empowers.

Faith is an elusive and questionable commodity in these days of a dying culture. Where do you find it? If you've lost a faith, can you invent one? Which faith to choose? Some of us have retained a faith in a just creator God or in a lawful, benevolent order to the universe. But some of us find it hard, even obscene, to believe in an abiding providence where, in the face of unimaginable suffering, much of our wealth and wits are employed in preparing a final holocaust. And we don't need nuclear bombs for that holocaust. It is going on right now in the demolition of the great rainforests and the toxic contamination of our seas, soil, and air, as well as the accelerating collapse of our planetary climate system.

In a world like this, what can faith mean? The very notion can appear distasteful, especially when we see faith widely used as an excuse for denial and inaction. "God won't let it happen."

Or even, in some circles, "It is God's will"—a fearful assertion when it refers to nuclear war as the final and holy battle to exterminate the wicked. The radical uncertainties of our time breed fundamentalism, self-righteousness, and deep divisions. These uncertainties turn patriotism into xenophobia, incite fear and hatred of dissenters, and fuel the engines of war.

Another option opens, however, that can lead to a more profound and authentic form of faith. We can turn from the search for personal salvation or some metaphysical haven, and look instead to our actual experience. When we simply attend to what we see, feel, and know is happening to our world, we find authenticity. Heading into a darkness where there appears to be little room for faith, we can still make three important discoveries. I see them as redeeming discoveries that can ground us in our ecology and serve as our faith. These three are: the discovery of what we know and feel, the discovery of what we are, and the discovery of what can happen through us.

DISCOVERING WHAT WE KNOW AND FEEL

To discover what we know and feel is not as easy as it sounds, because a great deal of effort in contemporary society is devoted to distracting us from the truth of our own experience. Entire industries are focused on persuading us that we are happy—or on the verge of being happy—as soon as we buy this toothpaste or that car. It is not in the interest of global corporations or governments or the media that serve them for us to become aware of our anguish with the way things are.

None of us, in our hearts, is free of sorrow for the suffering of other beings. None of us is indifferent to the dangers that threaten our planet's people or free of fear for the generations to come. Yet it is not easy to acknowledge what's happening, let alone give credence to the grief it engenders in a culture that enjoins us to "accentuate the positive."

The blocking of our natural responses to actual or impending disaster is endemic to our time, explains Robert Jay Lifton, the psychiatrist who pioneered the study of the psychological effects of nuclear weapons. The refusal to acknowledge these responses—or even feel them—produces a dangerous splitting. It divorces our mental calculations from our intuitive, emotional, and biological responses. That split allows us passively to acquiesce in preparations for our own demise.

This first discovery, opening to what we know and feel, takes courage. Like Gandhi's *satyagraha*, it involves "truth-force." People are not going to find their truth-force, or inner authority, by listening to the so-called experts, but by listening to themselves. Every one of us is an expert on what it is like to live on an endangered planet.

To affirm that expertise and counter habits of repression, a form of group work has evolved. In the Work That Reconnects, people come together to find their own inner authority. Without mincing words, without apology, embarrassment, or fear of distressing each other, they simply tell the truth about their experience of today's world. A young man talks about the dead fish in a stream he loves; a young couple wonders about the strontium-90 in the bones of their children. To quote Justin Kenrick, a colleague in this work: "We need permission in our minds and hearts and guts to accept that we are destroying the Earth and to feel the reality of who we are in that context; isolated, desperate, and powerless individuals, defeated by our old patterns of behavior before we have even begun to try to heal our lives and the Earth. Only then can we give ourselves permission to feel the power our culture denies us."[1]

In acknowledging our pain for the world, we return once more to the original meaning of *compassion:* "to suffer with." Suffering with our world, we are drawn into the cauldron of compassion. It awaits us, and it is there that we can reconnect with our roots and our power.

DISCOVERING WHAT WE ARE

Acknowledging the depths and reaches of our own inner experience, we come to the second discovery: the discovery of who and what we are. We are bearers of compassion. Buddhism has a term for that kind of being—it is the bodhisattva—the one with the boundless heart. The bodhisattvas know there is no private salvation. They do not hold aloof from this suffering world or try to escape from it, but return again and again to act on behalf of all beings.

According to Buddhist teachings, we are all, in essence, bodhisattvas. Our fundamental interconnections are represented in the beautiful image of the Jeweled Net of Indra. It is similar to the holographic model of the universe we find in contemporary science. In the cosmic canopy of Indra's Net, each of us is like a multifaceted jewel at each node of the net. Every jewel reflects all the others and catches what the others are reflecting back. We discover ourselves through what we awaken in others. Tears over the wars we make are not ours alone; they are also those of an Iraqi mother looking for her children in the rubble or those of a Black father whose son was just shot by the police.

We find ourselves as interwoven threads in the tapestry of our deep ecology.

What happens for us then is akin to what every major religion has offered in its way—a shift in identification from the isolated "I" to a vaster sense of being. This seems to be the direction of our evolution. As an evolving species, we shed our shells, our armor, our separate encasements; we became more soft and vulnerable by developing sensitive eyes, ears, lips, fingertips—the better to connect and receive information, the better to share and interweave our learnings. If, as the Buddha-dharma says, we are all bodhisattvas, it is because that thrust to connect, that capacity to integrate with and through each other, is how we are made.

Yet we are agonizingly slow to realize the truth of our mutual belonging. In his book *Ecology and Man*, Paul Shepard writes: "We are hidden from ourselves by patterns of perception. Our thought forms, our language, encourage us to see ourselves or a plant or an animal as an isolated sac, a thing, a contained self, whereas the epidermis of the skin is ecologically like a pond surface or a forest soil, not a shell so much as a delicate interpenetration." Paul Shepard is calling us to a faith in our very biology. He states it simply: "Affirmation of its own organic essence will be the ultimate test of the human mind."[2]

We begin to see that a shift of identification can release us not only from the prison cell of ego but also from loneliness as a species. As John Seed, founder of the Rainforest Information Centre in Australia, points out, it takes us "beyond anthropocentrism." In his essay of that title, he says that anthropocentrism or human chauvinism is similar to sexism, but substitute

"human race" for "men" and "all other species" for "women."
He goes on to say:

> When humans investigate and see through their layers of
> anthropocentric self-cherishing, a most profound change in
> consciousness begins to take place. Alienation subsides. The
> human is no longer an outsider apart. Your humanness is then
> recognized as being merely the most recent stage of your
> existence; as you stop identifying exclusively with this chap-
> ter, you start to get in touch with yourself as vertebrate, as
> mammal, as species only recently emerged from the rainfor-
> est. As the fog of amnesia disperses, there is a transformation
> in your relationship to other species and in your commitment
> to them. . . . The thousands of years of imagined separation
> are over, and we can begin to recall our true nature; that is, the
> change is a spiritual one—thinking like a mountain, sometimes
> referred to as deep ecology. As your memory improves . . .
> there is an identification with all life. . . . Remember our child-
> hood as rocks, as lava? Rocks contain the potentiality to weave
> themselves into such stuff as this. We are the rocks dancing.[3]

BEING ACTED THROUGH

That leads us to the third discovery offered to us by the deep
ecology of our lives. It is the discovery of what can happen
through us. If we are the rocks dancing, then the force that
evolved us from those rocks carries us forward now and sustains us in our work for the continuance of life.

When I admired a nurse for her strength and devotion
in keeping long hours on the COVID floors, she shrugged off
my compliment as if it were entirely misplaced. "It's not *my*
strength, you know. I get it from the life in *them*," she said,
nodding at the rows of beds. "They give me what I need to keep

going." Whether tending a garden or cooking in a soup kitchen, there is the sense of being sustained by something beyond one's own individual power—of being acted "through." It is close to the religious concept of grace, but unlike the traditional Western understanding of grace, it does not require belief in God or a supernatural agency. One simply finds oneself empowered to act on behalf of other beings or on behalf of the larger whole. The power itself seems to come through that or those for whose sake one acts. In the ecological context, this phenomenon is similar to understandings of synergy and symbiosis. It helps us re-conceptualize our very notion of what power is.

From the ecological perspective, all open systems—be they cells or organisms, cedars or swamps—are seen to be self-organizing. They don't require any external or superior agency to regulate them, any more than your liver or an apple tree needs direction on how to function. In other words, order, or dynamic self-organizing, is integral to life.

This contrasts with the hierarchical worldview that dominated our mainstream assumptions for millennia, where mind is set above nature and where order is assumed to be imposed from above on otherwise random stuff. We have tended to define power in the same way, seeing it as imposed from above. So we have equated power with domination, with one thing exerting its will over another in a zero-sum or win-lose game, where to be powerful means to resist the demands of another, and strong defenses are necessary to maintain one's advantage.

In falling into this way of thinking, we lose sight of the fact that this is not the way nature works. Living systems evolve in complexity, flexibility, and intelligence through interaction with each other. These interactions require openness and vulnerability in order to process the flow-through of energy and information, bringing new responses and possibilities into play. This collaborative release of novelty and fresh potential is called *synergy*. It is like grace, because it brings a reach and increase of power beyond one's individual capacity.

SUSTAINING OUR FAITH

What can we do to nourish these efforts and strengthen the bodhisattva in ourselves? Two ways that I know are through community and practice. Liberation struggles in Latin America and the Philippines have demonstrated the efficacy of spiritually based communities for nonviolent action. These tough networks of trust arise on the neighborhood level, as people strive together to understand, in their own terms and for their own situation, what they need to do to live without fear and injustice. These groups are just ordinary people meeting regularly in a discipline of honest searching and mutual commitment.

In our own society, too, such communities have been arising in the form of local support and mutual aid groups. Here neighbors or coworkers, parents or professionals organize and meet regularly to support each other in action—be it through growing food together or preparing as a neighborhood for climate-driven emergencies like fires and flooding. Those of us who participate in such team efforts know that they enhance both personal integrity and our belief in what is possible.

In addition to such external support, we need, in this time of great challenge, the internal support of personal practice. I mean *practice* in the spiritual sense, of fortifying the mind and schooling its attitudes. For generations we have been conditioned by mechanistic, anthropocentric assumptions, so intellectual assent to an ecological vision of life is not enough to change our perceptions and behaviors. The heart-mind needs to be trained to decondition our responses that are based on narrow notions of the self. The imagination needs to be schooled in order to experience our deep ecology in the web of life.

Spiritual exercises for cultivating reverence for life and building solidarity are increasingly necessary to sustain our commitments and energy. Practices of many traditions are now being welcomed by people regardless of their religious affiliation. I have found adaptations from Buddhist practices particularly helpful, because they are grounded in the recognition of the interdependent co-arising or deep ecology of all things. (See examples in the back of this book.)

OUR MUTUAL BELONGING

I am remembering now that gray morning in the meadow with those ancient standing stones. It was over three decades ago, but I imagine I can still hear the voices of the men and women gathered there. In that final hour of our Deep Ecology week, they were speaking in turn, finding words for actions and life-style changes they felt called to make for the health and healing of our world.

My mind opens to what has arisen in the United Kingdom in the intervening years and flashes on developments that no one would have expected—the closing, finally, of the last nuclear air base at Greenham Common, the birth and growth of the Transition Town movement, the stunning emergence of Extinction Rebellion, and the Deep Adaptation forum helping me and others around the world find vision in the acceptance of economic collapse.

When I think of these feisty, inventive campaigns and the spirit that ignites them, I wonder if it's not, in some way, the same spirit that moved through the words spoken back then around the standing stones—a spirit, both ancient and new, arising from the realization of our mutual belonging in the living body of Earth.

THIRTEEN

IN LEAGUE WITH THE BEINGS OF THE FUTURE

Every being who will ever live on Earth is here right now.
Where? In our ovaries and gonads, and in our DNA.

—SPOKEN BY SISTER ROSALIE BERTELL

I remember a verse of the Bible that delighted me as a child and stayed with me as I grew up. It was from the book of Job: *For thou shalt be in league with the stones of the field, and the beasts of the field shall be at peace with thee.*

It promised a way I wanted to live—in complicity with creation. It still comes to mind when I hear about people taking action on behalf of our living Earth. When our brothers and sisters at Standing Rock keep the sacred flame burning for water protectors to come, I think, "Ah, they are in league." And when indigenous elders of the Amazon speak out for their rainforest, I think, "Ah, they, too, are in league."

To be "in league" in that way seems wonderful. There is a comfortable, cosmic collegiality to it—like coming home to conspire once more with our beloved and age-old companions, with the ancient trees and the great beings of the ocean, with the sun that rises and the stars revolving in the sky.

Now the work of restoring our ravaged Earth offers us that—with a new dimension. It not only puts us in league with the trees, whales, microbes, and fungi, but also in league with the beings of the future. All that we do to mend our planet is for their sake, too. Their chance to be alive and love our world depends in large measure on us and our uncertain efforts.

Sister Rosalie Bertell, radiologist renowned for her research and testimony on radioactive contamination from nuclear energy and weapons production, made it clear that all future beings on Earth will be impacted by the mutating toxins that we are absorbing now, affecting our DNA. My growing concerns about this toxic legacy, especially its duration—lasting for thousands and even millions of generations—has deepened my sense of connection with all who come after us.

The beings of the future and their claim on life have come to seem so real to me that I sometimes sense them hovering, like a cloud of witnesses. Sometimes I fancy that if I were to turn my head suddenly, I would glimpse them over my shoulder. Their imagined presence gives context and impetus to our work for a nuclear-free world.

In that context it is plausible to me that the generations of the future want to lend us courage for what we do. I imagine them saying *thank you* for our efforts to keep mines from leaching toxins into rivers and topsoil from blowing away. Thanks for our citizen campaigns on behalf of a safe climate. Thank you, ancestors, for working on renewable energy, so that we have clean air to breathe.

The imagined presence of these future ones comes to me like grace and works upon my life. They are why I have been drawn, almost despite myself, to the difficult issue of radioactive waste. In terms of time and toxicity, it is the most enduring legacy our generation will leave behind.

AWAKENED BY DREAMS

For many of us, our dream life now includes frightening scenes of the future. We rise from bed haunted by images of tidal waves, wasted landscapes, and social chaos. These nightmares arise from the collective psyche, warning us of dangers that are still easy to shun in our waking lives. They challenge us to incorporate their content into conscious awareness and free them from the grip of unconscious forces. As C. G. Jung explained, if we repress subliminal fears, intimated in our dreams, they are more likely to be acted out on the stage of history.

In the late 1970s, I had such a dream. At the time, I was taking part in a citizens' lawsuit to stop the faulty storage of high-level waste at a nearby nuclear reactor. My task, as the only non-lawyer on our team, was to review and summarize public health statistics in order to substantiate our legal claims. At the Nuclear Regulatory Commission, whose library was still open then to public access, I pored over statistics revealing mounting incidence of miscarriages, birth defects, and leukemia and other cancers in the proximity of nuclear plants. Learning that genetic damage would compound over time, I strained to conceive of *spans* of time like a quarter million years, the hazardous life of plutonium, such as that created at the power station we were concerned about. One night, before going to bed, I leafed through photos of our three children to find a snapshot for my daughter's high school yearbook.

In the dream, I behold the three of them as they appeared in the old photos, and am struck most by the sweet wholesomeness of their flesh. My husband and I are journeying with them across an unfamiliar landscape. The terrain becomes dreary, treeless, and strewn with rocks; little Peggy can barely clamber over the boulders in the path. Just as the going is getting difficult, even frightening, I suddenly realize that by some thoughtless but unalterable prearrangement, their father and I must leave them. I can see the grimness of the way that lies ahead for them, bleak as a red moonscape and with a flesh-burning sickness in the air. I am maddened by sorrow that my children must face this without me. I kiss each one and tell them we will meet again, but I know no place to name where we will meet. Perhaps another planet, I say. Innocent of terror, they try to reassure me, ready to be off. Removed, and from a height in the sky, I watch them go—three small solitary figures trudging across that angry wasteland, holding each other by the hand and not stopping to look back. In spite of the widening distance, I see, with a surrealist's precision, the ulcerating of their flesh. I see how the skin bubbles and curls back to expose raw tissue as they doggedly go forward, the boys helping their little sister across the rocks.

I woke up, brushed my teeth, showered, and tried to wash those images away. But when I roused Peggy for school, I sank beside her bed. "Hold me," I said, "I had a bad dream." I sobbed against her body, as the knowledge of all that assails it surfaced in me. The statistical studies on the effects of ionizing radiation, the dry columns of figures, their import beyond utterance, turned now to wracking tears.

Our citizens' group lost its suit against the Virginia Electric Power Company, but it taught me a lot. It taught me that all children for centuries to come are my children. It taught me about the misuse of our technology and the obscenity of the legacy it bequeaths future generations—lessons confirmed over and over again by exposés of mismanagement, accidents, and spills at nuclear installations. "Temporarily" stored in pools and corrodible containers, they leak into air, soil, aquifers, and rivers, while the only long-term solution still considered by government and industry is burial—deep in the ground—which makes it impossible to monitor and repair the containers.

THE POISON FIRE AS TEACHER

From the perspective of future generations, this policy—to put the waste out of sight and out of mind—amounts to betrayal. As we discover in other aspects of our lives, hiding doesn't work in the long run. This is especially true of nuclear materials, because, irradiated by their contents, containers corrode. As Earth's strata shift and water seeps, the radioactivity spreads—into aquifers, into the biosphere, into lungs and wombs.

A different approach to nuclear waste had occurred to me in Great Britain in the early 1980s, when I visited Greenham Common and other citizen encampments surrounding US nuclear missile bases. I sensed immediately their commitment to the future. With their unflagging dedication and strong spiritual flavor, these "peace camps" called to mind the monasteries that kept the lamp of learning alive through the Dark Ages. I realized then that steadfast people with similar dedication would be needed to guard the centers of radioactivity we are bequeathing to tens of thousands of future generations.

In my mind's eye, I could see surveillance communities forming around today's nuclear facilities. I imagined I saw guardian sites—centers of reflection and pilgrimage, where waste containers were monitored and repaired, and where wisdom traditions of our planetary heritage offered contexts of meaning and disciplines of vigilance. Here, "remembering" would be undertaken—the crucial task of understanding the origins and nature of this radioactivity, as well as ongoing mindfulness of its danger. Here, those who came for varying periods of time would participate in an active learning community—to receive training and take their turn at nuclear guardianship.

The vision stayed with me. Recruiting colleagues, I formed a study-action group on nuclear waste to comprehend the dangers in current practices and the requirements for responsible long-term care. A similar group formed in Germany. Desiring throughout to be "in league with the beings of the future," we invited them to our sessions through invocations and prayerful listening, scenario games and role plays. We first heard the future ones' name for our radioactive legacy in a simulation game: they call it *the poison fire*.

Our study-action group soon addressed the wider public in an educational endeavor called the Nuclear Guardianship Project. To promote on-site, retrievable storage of nuclear waste, we published an annual newspaper for three years and testified at regulatory hearings. We also presented to churches, schools, and any organization that invited us. As I recall some of those many presentations, I am awed by their creative audacity, as they conveyed—with music, projected images, and enactments—the perspective and needs of future generations.

We wanted the future ones to become as real to others as they were to us. We wanted to share the teachings we had received from them, words like this:

> *You, in whose generation the poison fire was made, you have some obligations. You need technical training in radiation and protection from it. You need moral training as well, in the vigilance required to keep it out of the biosphere. No containment lasts as long as the poison fire itself. You cannot hide it and walk away. But so long as you pay attention, so long as it's kept visible to the watchful eye and accessible for repair, you will be guardians—and you will pass that learning on to us. To carry that responsibility through the chaos to come, faithful commitment is essential—and community to sustain it. So begin now.*

One of the splendid things about living into my tenth decade is having the joy of working in league with some of the future guardians I had imagined at Greenham Common. Among them is my friend Eileen O'Shaughnessy, a beautiful singer-songwriter and activist, who is the many-times great-granddaughter of the Irish pirate rebel Grace O'Malley. Eileen is a lecturer at the University of New Mexico, where she teaches an undergraduate course she designed for the Sustainability Studies program, called "Nuclear New Mexico."

"At the heart of nuclear issues," Eileen reflects, "is an invitation and necessity to see beyond our limited view of time." Eileen sees this as an alliance with future beings—a two-way street. And she seems to be here just for this task, awakening in millennial students the capacity to be nuclear guardians and carry this mission into the future.

Her semester-long course is an exploration of social and environmental justice along the nuclear fuel chain. There is a lot to cover, and uncover, about New Mexico's seventy-eight-year toxic history with nuclear technology. New Mexico built the first nuclear laboratory, made the first nuclear warhead, exploded the first nuclear bomb, built the bomb that was dropped on Hiroshima, dug uranium mines all over the Navajo Nation, experienced the first mega nuclear spill (at Church Rock), and created, at Carlsbad, the first US geological repository for nuclear waste, where leakage required extended closure. And now, high-level nuclear waste loaded on trains and barges is planned to arrive from every direction across the United States to be deposited at two sites near low-income rural communities, one in southeastern New Mexico and another just across the border in Texas.

As Eileen guides her students into the course, it's as if she's lifting a veil, and the students are experiencing an initiation. To take the poison fire as our teacher—to hear the stories, visit the sites, and integrate the knowledge of its impacts and not look away—is to be forever changed. You are forever changed, because you are seized by a life purpose in service to Earth and held by a lineage of activists and guardians dedicated to this task. Though we split the atom without the wisdom to care for it, the poison fire teaches us to be awake, to be faithful, and to never forget. As her students head out the door into that vast New Mexico sky, Eileen calls out her favorite parting words: "Stay safe, be well, raise hell."

PRACTICING GUARDIANSHIP

This call is being heeded, not just in specific sites of contamination, but as a principle to uphold in every aspect of our lives.

Take the precautionary principle, for example, and see how quickly it has entered public discourse and policy. Developed by scientists and lawyers in the Science and Environmental Health Network (SEHN), the precautionary principle draws on the German concept of *Vorsorge*, "forecare," to serve as an economic and legal framework that takes into account the potential harm of any human activity. Carolyn Raffensperger, one of SEHN's founding visionaries, calls it plain common sense or the "grandmother principle"—"better safe than sorry," "an ounce of prevention is worth a pound of cure," "a stitch in time saves nine." It reverses the burden of proof from those who may be harmed to those who propose new developments and technologies—be they untested chemicals, genetically modified organisms, or the siting of industrial plants. The precautionary principle requires us to explore the range of safe alternatives, including no action at all.

Writer Terry Tempest Williams defines this concept as "restraint in the name of reverence." Global recommendations for energy policy and climate solutions today all draw strongly on the precautionary principle, aiming to reduce harm to future generations as much as possible. Likewise, organic food production and complementary medicine take this principle as a starting point for their work.

Based on this principle, SEHN developed guidelines for future generation guardianship that could be applied in challenging environmental situations. Working with Bob Shimek of the Indigenous Environmental Network, SEHN found a way to link the precautionary principle with the native seventh-generation principle in addressing impacts from the proposed "Giant Mine" at Bristol Bay, Alaska. At twenty square miles, this is slated to be one of the largest open-pit gold mines in the world. They came up with a strategy to designate a legal guardian to protect the interests and rights of future generations. As Raffensperger described it, this legal provision would align rights of nature with rights of future generations, supporting the seventh-generation principle for all beings in formal frameworks such as constitutional law.

The Indigenous Environmental Network (IEN), as a grassroots coalition, has advocated for such rights on behalf of native peoples around the globe. In its Bemidji Statement of 2006, the IEN brought the following questions to the designation of Guardians for the Seventh Generation:

Who guards this web of life that nurtures and sustains us all?
Who watches out for the land, the sky, the fire, and the water?
Who watches out for our relatives that swim, fly, walk, or crawl?
Who watches out for the plants that are rooted in
our Mother Earth?
Who watches out for the life-giving spirits that reside
in the underworld?
Who tends the languages of the people and the land?
Who tends the children and the families?
Who tends the peacekeepers in our communities?[1]

The late Walter Bresette, IEN member and a leader of the Anishinaabe nation, had these questions in mind when he drafted a constitutional amendment granting rights to future beings. His proposal, called the "Amendment for the Seventh Generation" states: "The right of citizens of the United States to use and enjoy air, water, wildlife, and other renewable resources determined by the Congress to be common property shall not be impaired, nor shall such use impair their availability for the use of future generations."[2] This amendment would write the protection of the commons into the US Constitution, which does not yet include any rights to a clean environment.

Dallas Goldtooth, son of Tom Goldtooth, one of the founders of IEN, now heads up a guardianship project, the "Keep it in the Ground Campaign." Goldtooth was a lead Water Protector at Standing Rock/Oceti Sakowin Camp, fighting the Dakota Access Pipeline. His vision of a fossil fuel–free and climate-safe future, with safe water for all, calls for a powerful sense of moral imagination and moral courage.

If we are to protect conditions for life on Earth, then we are called to become guardians of our climate. Our guardianship practice means securing global, national, and local commitments to reduce fossil fuel use and cut greenhouse gas emissions. Don't be misled by arguments that nuclear energy is somehow safer, that it does not generate climate pollution. Every step of the nuclear fuel chain—from the mining, milling, and hauling of the uranium ore to the construction of the reactors and use of storage pools generates plenty of greenhouse gas emissions. The dangers are clear: we must take our guardianship knowledge with us as we consider the impacts on generations to come from greenhouse gases, as well as radioactivity.

FAZANG AND THE THREE TIMES

So many opportunities are opening now to play our part in a story that extends through time. As I reflect on this, I am inspired by an ancient teacher of the Dharma. Living fourteen centuries ago, Fazang was a scholar of the Hua Yen scriptures of Mahayana Buddhism. These offer elaborate descriptions and imagery to convey the Buddha's teaching of interdependent co-arising. Vast cosmic scenes spanning all space and time—peopled with astronomical numbers of beings and bodhisattvas—unfold the logic of that teaching to reveal the relatedness of all phenomena, their interpenetration as well. An image conveying that radical mutuality, like an early version of today's holographic view of the universe, is the Jeweled Net of Indra. The fabric of the universe is conceived as a vast net that holds, at every node, a multifaceted jewel. And each jewel mirrors all the other jewels back and forth, generating an infinite dance of reflection.

The empress of China was so fascinated by the Hua Yen scriptures that she ordered all eighty volumes to be translated from the Sanskrit. She often came in person to the monastery where the scholars were at work, bringing them food and drink. To celebrate the completion of the project, she invited Master Fazang to the palace to preach about Indra's Net and the interpenetration of all phenomena. She thanked him for his brilliance and then asked for something more.

"You have explained the teaching to me with great clarity," she said. "Sometimes I can almost see the vast truth of it in my mind's eye. But all this, I realize, is still conjecture." She reminded Fazang of the Buddha's insistence that direct experience was more reliable than inference, and she asked him for an experiential teaching. "Can you give me a demonstration that will reveal the great truth of all-in-one and one-in-all?"

A few days later Fazang escorted the empress to the demonstration he had prepared for her in one of the palace rooms. Mirrors were fixed to its four walls and corners, as well as the ceiling and floor. Then the scholar placed a small statue of the Buddha in the center of the room with a candle beside it.

"Oh, how marvelous!" cried the empress, beholding in awe the panorama of infinite reflections. And she thanked Fazang for helping her to know the great teaching not only with her intellect, but with her senses.

Afterward, the empress asked the great scholar if he could show in a similar physical fashion the interplay between past, present, and future. Fazang told her that such a demonstration might be possible to contrive. But it would be more difficult, he said, and he did not have the means at hand.

I want to step through time and tell the great teacher Fazang that we have managed to achieve it. In the radioactive legacy we have created, we have found a way to apprehend our immediate and unseverable connections with future generations. As Sister Rosalie Bertell pointed out, our present choices have a direct influence on whether beings born eons from today will be of sound mind and body. Our karma, the consequence of our actions, now extends into geological time periods—and even as long as Earth's life span to date, given the half-life of depleted uranium, which is 4.5 billion years.

This fact, by itself, chills the soul. But as I take it in, I hear Fazang reminding me that interdependent co-arising is a two-way street. In the mystery of time, the bonds we forge to future beings can bring them into our lives in ways unforeseen in the linear view. In our actions to serve life on Earth, we can feel them at our side, lending strength and counsel.

Sometimes I find myself praying, not only *for* them, but also *to* them. I ask them to help us be faithful in the work that we, their ancestors, have been given to do.

You live inside us, beings of the future.
In the spiral ribbons of our cells, you are here.
In our rage for the burning forests, the flooded fields,
    the fevered climate,
you are here.
You beat in our hearts through late-night meetings.
You accompany us to clearcuts and toxic dumps,
    to climate hearings and protests in the streets.
It is you who drive our dogged labors to save what
    is left.

O you, who will walk this Earth when we are gone,
    stir us awake.
Behold through our eyes the beauty of this world.
Let us feel your breath in our lungs, your cry in our throat.
Let us see you in the homeless, the wounded, the sick.
Haunt us with your hunger, hound us with your claims,
    that we may honor the life that links us.

You have as yet no faces we can see, no names we can say.
But we need only hold you in our mind, and you teach us
    patience.
You attune us to measures of time where healing can
    happen,
where soil and souls can mend.

You reveal courage within us we had not suspected,
love we had not owned.
O you who come after, help us remember: we are your
ancestors.
Fill us with gladness for the work that must be done.[3]

FOURTEEN

THE FULLNESS OF TIME

. . . to think in deep time can be a means
not of escaping our troubled present,
but rather of re-imagining it,
countermanding its quick greeds and furies
with older, slower stories of making and unmaking.

—ROBERT MACFARLANE

At about the same time that deep ecology and the group work
it inspired entered my life, I became preoccupied with the
challenge presented by nuclear waste and its long-term care.
By some kind of psychic synergy, these two concerns together
invited me to think about time in new ways. I became fascinated
by how we, as a culture, relate to time—and what that means
for life on Earth. It soon occurred to me that both our ongoing
destruction of our world and our ability to stop it are rooted in
the way we experience time.

I became persuaded that we of the industrial growth society are subject to a rare and probably unprecedented experience
of time. It can be likened to an ever-shrinking box in which we
race on a treadmill at increasingly frenetic speeds. Cutting us off
from other rhythms of life, this box cuts us off from past and

future as well. It blocks our perceptual field while allowing only the briefest experience of time.

Until we break out of this temporal trap, it will be hard for us to adequately address the crises we have created. But now, new perspectives emerge to indicate that we may be able to inhabit time in a healthier, saner fashion. By opening up our experience of time in organic, ecological, and geological terms, we would increase the chances of life continuing on Earth.

THE BROKEN CONNECTION

Our experience of time reveals a pathetically shrunken sense of time and a pathological denial of its continuity. This disregard for the future is all the more astonishing since it runs counter to our nature as biological systems. Living organisms are built to propagate and to invest a great deal of time and energy in the complex set of behaviors that effort requires. Through these behaviors, which usually have no direct survival value to the individual, the future is wired in. There is, as systems thinker Tyrone Cashman points out,

> this spilling out into the future that is the entire essence of organisms. Any plant or animal for whom, throughout its species history, this was not its most essential characteristic would not exist at all. This wired-in relationship to time is alterable only at the price of extinction. Of course, this time-thrust, this into-the-future-ness of all living beings can be lost by a species. But then, immediately, the species itself disappears, forever.[1]

This systems design common to all organisms is clearly evident throughout human history. At great personal cost, men and women have labored to create monuments of art, such as the great Mayan temples, and bodies of knowledge to endure far beyond their individual lives. It makes our present generation's disregard for the future appear amazing, indeed. What developments can account for it?

For one thing, the atomic bomb has happened. The advent of nuclear weapons has ruptured our sense of biological continuity and our felt connections with both past and future. Arguing this point, Robert J. Lifton says, "We need not enter the debate as to whether nuclear war would or would not eliminate *all* human life. The fact that there is such a debate in itself confirms the importance of *imagery* of total biological destruction, or radically impaired imagination of human continuity."[2]

This impairment reaches backward as well as forward, since, as he says, our sense of connection with prior generations "depends on feeling part of a continuing sequence of generations. The image of a destructive force of unlimited dimensions . . . enters into every relationship involving parents, children, grandparents, and imagined great-grandparents and great-grandchildren." Lifton concludes, "we are thus among the first to live with a recurrent sense of biological severance."[3]

From the thousands of people I've met in workshops, I know this to be true. When people feel safe to express their inner responses to the nuclear and ecological crises, it is the threats to all life that surface as their deepest and most pervasive anguish. This anguish is far greater than fears for their individual well-being. And now, with climate chaos erupting all around us, this has become even more widespread.

THE TIME SQUEEZE

While the pandemic has offered many of us a respite from haste and a speedy lifestyle, the rapidity with which people are flying again, despite orders or strong warnings, reflects an eagerness to return to the old normal. We have lived with crowded schedules and relentless pressure from commitments for so long that anything slower does not feel normal or even important. We are used to working hard to earn a few moments of ease and relaxation. Unless you are at the top of the capitalist economy, the corporate treadmill requires more and more of our time to stay afloat.

Before the pandemic, time itself, both as a commodity and an experience, had become a scarcity. It has been a painful irony that we who have more time-saving devices than any culture of the past appear the most time-harried and driven. The paradox is only apparent, however, for our time-scarcity is linked to the very time-efficiency of our technology. As Jeremy Rifkin chronicles in *Time Wars*, our measure of time—once based on the changing seasons and wheeling stars, and then the ticking of the clock—is now parceled out in computer nanoseconds; we have lost time as an organically measurable experience.

Larry Dossey, physician and author of *Space, Time and Medicine*, points out that this causes *hurry sickness*. "Our perceptions of speeding clocks and vanishing time cause our own biological clocks to speed. The end result is frequently some form of hurry sickness—expressed as heart disease, high blood pressure, or depression of our immune function, leading to an increased susceptibility to infection and cancer."[4]

The *Kali Yuga*, the "age of iron," is ancient India's name for the final degenerative era of a world cycle. One meaning of Kali Yuga is "the dregs of time," a temporal density we can imagine as gritty and bitter as used coffee grounds. In this final stage, time gets extreme, speeds up, clogs our pores.

Speed and haste, as many a wise one has pointed out, are inherently violent. The violence they inflict on our environment is not only because of our appetite for time-saving devices and the materials to make them but also because they put us out of sync with the ecosystem. The natural systems that sustain us move at slower rhythms than we do. The feedback loops are longer and take more time than our interactions with machines. In the rush of minutes and seconds, we don't notice the slow increments of sea level rise or the changing length of seasons. Our own accelerating speed distances us ever more from the rhythms of the natural world and blinds us to our impact upon it.

YEARNING TO ESCAPE FROM TIME

Like many of my friends, I've learned to find release from haste by practices such as meditation. Relaxing into the rhythm of breathing in and breathing out, I let the pressures of the day drop away. This behavior can be helpful in slowing us down a bit, but it may imply that time is an enemy to be conquered or outwitted. Some Buddhist teachers use the teaching of impermanence to point to the unsatisfactoriness of life. What you cherish soon passes. Flowers wilt, paint peels, lovers leave, your own body sags, wrinkles, and decays. Ah, woe! Better fix your gaze on what is free from the ravages of time.

At a gathering of dharma friends in the mid-1980s, when I was preoccupied with nuclear waste, I asked each person to reflect on their experience of time and if they could see ways to support a wider temporal context for our lives. Everyone spoke with great feeling about the frenzied and fragmented pace of daily life. When I invited them to hypothesize alternatives to these pressures, only one was suggested: escape into timelessness. The only remedy they saw was to cultivate an experience of eternity aloof from chronological time.

This bothered me a lot, because I was seeking ways to imagine and enlist ongoing guardianship of nuclear waste. I was looking for ways to relate to time that could help us face up to the challenge of that incredibly long-lived radioactivity. I wanted us to find the ability to inhabit time in longer stretches, not escape from it altogether.

A key feature of our capacity to make nuclear war is speed. The technological design thrust is to accelerate response to attack and to make launch-on-warning as instantaneous as possible. The time allowed for human appraisal and intervention—to see, for example, if the attack is real or the result of a computer misreading—has been continually reduced. Our nuclear missiles may be the logical unfolding of our "spiritual" desire to escape from time. So let us ask, how can we move beyond our fear of time so that our days on Earth may be long?

When I realized the longevity of nuclear waste, it was as though time turned inside out. It wasn't a question any more of how much we can accomplish in a small amount of time, but how long we can continue to do the same thing. How can we *sustain* our attention on the poison fire? If you just take that into your chest, it alters your metabolism. Can you feel that?

SATURN TIME

One November morning back in the time of our guardianship meetings, I awoke from a dream—or rather with a dream, for it has accompanied me ever after. In the dream, I have undertaken a mission to alert the rest of our solar system to a peril we have fallen into on Earth. The mission is not to seek help so much as to report a situation that our neighbors need to know about; it is of crucial importance that we somehow face this together. I have just returned home from a visit to the planet Mercury. Orbiting nearer to the sun, its tempo is faster than ours. Like that of a hummingbird, the metabolism of Mercury's beings is quite rapid, and for me to communicate with them had been somewhat exhausting. I still feel the effects of that speed and frenzy, like a caffeine jag, as I prepare for the next and far more difficult venture.

I am getting ready to go to Saturn, which will be the greatest challenge of all. That is because, being so distant from our sun, time on Saturn is extremely slow for a being from Earth. I get a briefing from those who have assigned me to this mission. I am told the time ratio: two and a half minutes of Saturnian time will last a whole hour for me; an hour for them is a full day and night for me. Therefore, communicating with the beings there will require great steadiness of attention, far beyond anything I have ever attempted. I understand that if my attention falters for an instant, I will be incinerated by my own speediness and distraction—like a puff of oxygen in an alien atmosphere—and the beings of Saturn will hardly notice.

In my briefing, as if on a screen, I am accorded a glimpse of them. They are somber, faceless, and very tall, like dark columns moving through the mist. Their world has the grim, harsh austerity of ancient Sparta. Compared to them, we Earthlings are like frenzied insects, buzzing in erratic, mindless pursuits. The Saturnians' tempo is synchronized with the long-term unfolding of actions; they emanate a remorseless inevitability. Without pity or humor, they would as easily see me die as I would swat a fly. I fear them, and I fear our contact more than anything I have ever faced.

It is not clear whether such a venture between our worlds has succeeded before, and I realize there is a good possibility I will not return. In the dream, Fran, my husband, knows this too, but he does not try to hold me back. Though this is clearly my mission, not his, I feel his support and respect. There is in me no question about whether I will go; more than our own survival seems at stake.

It occurs to me that I have a chance of performing and surviving the mission if I can manage to trust firmly in the determination of my heart. Not my intellect, but only pure, unflinching, heartfelt intention can hold me sufficiently steady. So, I practice it as I prepare. I find it isn't hard if I hold firm to my love for the world and believe it. When I do, I can feel an actual physical warmth in my chest, like a tiny furnace. Though vulnerable, this love is clearly the only reliable protection. I am glad it can go with me.

Now it's time to go. I say goodbye to Fran and enter the underground way to Saturn. It is the entrance to the Aeroport metro stop in Moscow. The wide stairway leads down to a broad, dim marble corridor. There are others moving along in the same direction toward the transit point for Saturn; the waiting cars are still out of sight. I am surprised to see these people, because I had assumed I would be going alone. Walking along near me is a man with a little boy. The father is talking to his son, reminding him about the difference in tempo he will encounter on Saturn and repeating the same time ratio. Two and a half minutes for them is an hour for us, an hour for them is a full day and night for us. The warm kindness in his voice melts some of my fear. Ah, I think, how much easier it is when people talk about what they're facing. I keep on walking into the gloom toward the cars for Saturn, and though I do not speak, I feel less afraid.

At that point I woke up. I never found out if I could communicate with the slow, somber minds of Saturn. Just as well, I thought, I would probably need the rest of my life to learn how. Though the dream itself was scary, its effect on me seemed both steadying and strangely liberating. It left me feeling that I had one foot in another dimension, or as if there were or could be an alongside life not chopped up into fleeting moments, but extending in limitless continuities of time. Rilke's lines from his *Book of Hours* came back to me.

I love the dark hours of my being.
My mind deepens into them.
There I can find, as if in old letters, the days of my life,
Already lived and held like a legend.
Then the knowing comes: I can open to another life
That's wide and timeless.[5]

The wide and timeless seemed more real now and more close at hand—which was a relief, because I was accustomed to hurrying. I forever lacked time for all I needed to do. And even when I actually had plenty of time, say climbing a mountain or sitting down with a book, the habit of haste could catch up with me. Now time turned inside out. The Saturn dream reminded me that the challenge of guarding our everlasting nuclear waste was the reverse of hurry. It was no longer a question of how many things to squeeze into a short time span, but how to do one thing for a very long time. Could I be faithful to one task, if I literally had all the time in the world? Could I commit to it, if my lifespan were but one thousandth of that task's duration?

Saturn, as I recalled after the dream, is mythically and archetypally identified as Chronos. As such, it represents the impact and temporal consequences of the actions we choose to take, and our accountability for them—or justice. As the Buddha made clear, it is our intended actions that shape the person we become. In Saturn we can recognize not only Chronos but also the face of justice.

Nuclear waste is a bridge to the far future. It extends the effects of our actions, our karma, into the thousands and even millions of years that their hazardous life entails. When the longevity of nuclear toxicity dawned on me, I glimpsed what this challenge would mean in terms of sustained human attention. Now the demands of time reversed themselves. The question of *how fast* one could get something done was replaced with the question of *how long*—how *lo-o-n-n-ng*—one could keep on doing it. Will we actually be able to remember the lethal toxicity of these wastes and protect ourselves for a hundred years, a thousand, or a hundred thousand? As I pondered the likelihood of this, the challenge became duration, not speed, the long haul, not the quick move—in other words, *faithfulness*. My breath slowed, my rib cage eased. The horror of nuclear waste was inviting me to inhabit the fullness of time.

SPEAKING FOR THE FUTURE

If, for a livable world, we must learn to reinhabit time, what changes might be required in our system of self-governance?

What political practices could reflect and encourage a sense of responsibility to coming generations? Could we create structures to give voice to the interests of future generations? Since we are taxing future generations by exploiting their resources, they should have their say in the process. This would be totally in keeping with our principle of no taxation without representation. Because they are not born yet or too young to vote, offices could be instituted for statements to be made on their behalf.

One possibility has a precedent in the congressional offices of representatives of Puerto Rico and the District of Columbia. Though without a legislative vote, they are provided the means to bring views and needs of their constituencies to the attention of Congress. In my mind's eye, I picture a similar non-voting representative for the People of the Future to bring their perspectives and needs into legislative debates. This representative could be selected at a special convention in Washington, which would, in itself, be a salutary exercise in raising awareness of the effects of our present policies on coming generations. Such a law has already been passed in Wales, the Well-Being of Future Generations Act 2015, which "requires public bodies in Wales to think about the long-term impact of their decisions, to work better with people, communities and each other, and to prevent persistent problems such as poverty, health inequalities and climate change."[6]

A second possibility has even greater potential for changing our society's consciousness of time. Consider the establishment of a third house of Congress, a House of Spokespersons for the Future. Though without the power to pass laws, it would speak for the rights of coming generations. Its members, or

"Spokes," would be high school seniors, two from each state, chosen at statewide conventions on congressional election years. The House of Spokes could convene in Washington as needed, evaluate bills before Congress, and suggest new legislation. Across the year, its members would still be heard from, as they speak for the priorities they see asappropriate for a healthy and decent future.

When I see the student leaders for Fridays for the Future in different countries, their intelligence and determination inspired by Greta Thunberg, I am convinced of the role they can play in securing our shared future. When I watch the young people becoming global ambassadors for climate, they reveal to me a force for the future that this time now offers us. When I hear of climate suits such as *Youth v. Gov*, I know their actions will shape legal arguments to come. With all these young people driving the future forward, I feel the fullness of time inside me, and I know we belong to the regenerating dance of this planet.

PART FOUR

Food
for the
Journey

FIFTEEN

THE GREAT TURNING

Another world is not only possible, she is on her way.
On a quiet day, I can hear her breathing.

—ARUNDHATI ROY

The turning wheel is a powerful symbol of the mystery at the heart of life. Planets, solar systems, and electrons in their orbits are wheels revolving within larger wheels, just as the hours and seasons of day and year rotate. As blood circulates through the body, so do vast hydrological and carbon cycles sustain our living world. Like the sacred hoop of Native Americans and the round dances and mandalas of ancient peoples, the wheel reminds us that all is alive and moving, interconnected and intersecting. Little wonder, then, that the wheel has served to symbolize the Dharma. For the Buddha taught, in his central doctrine, the interdependent co-arising of all things, how they continually change and condition each other in interconnections as real as the spokes in a wheel. Thus, when he taught, he was said to turn the Wheel of the Dharma.

Earlier I described two turnings of the Wheel of the Dharma. The first turning occurred when the Buddha started teaching radical interdependence of all things. The second occurred at the beginning of the Mahayana, when scriptures honoring the Perfection of Wisdom, or Mother of All Buddhas, returned to that central doctrine and recast it in new perspectives and fresh forms. Now, I suggest, the cognitive shifts and spiritual openings taking place in our own time can be seen as another turning of the Wheel, a reawakening, at last, to our interdependence and mutual belonging.

The recognition of our essential non-separateness from the world, beyond the shaky walls erected by our fear and greed, is a gift occurring in countless lives in every generation. Yet there are historical moments when this recognition breaks through on a more collective level. This is happening now in ways that converge to bring into question the very foundation and direction of civilization. With the paradigm shift ignited by systems thinking and quantum science in the mid-twentieth century, our perceptions of reality deepened and expanded dramatically. Now, in the early years of the new millennium, this paradigm shift feeds into the climate movement, the racial justice movement, and our journey with the pandemic. This global revolution is of such magnitude that people unacquainted with Buddhism are using a similar term: many are calling it the Great Turning.

TOWARD A LIFE-SUSTAINING SOCIETY

Corporate-controlled media are not reporting this tidal change, but once we learn to see it, our time in history no longer appears as some grim, hopeless fate. It becomes a great adventure that can invigorate and ennoble every aspect of life. It is the epochal shift of allegiance and purpose from the industrial growth society to a life-sustaining society. And it is a matter of survival.

This revolution begins with the acknowledgment of two facts. First, that an economic system that depends on ever-increasing corporate profits—on how fast the earth can be turned into consumer goods, weapons, and waste—is suicidal. And second, that our needs can be met without destroying our world. We have the technology and resources available to produce sufficient food and energy, ensure clean air and water, and leave a livable world for those who come after us.

Future generations—if we leave them the means to exist—may look back on the twenty-first century as the time of Great Turning. I imagine they might say, "Those ancestors back then, bless them. Though working to save life on Earth, they had no way of knowing if they could pull it off. It must have looked hopeless at times. Their efforts must have often seemed isolated, diffuse, darkened by confusion. Yet they went ahead—they kept on doing what they could—and because they kept on, the Great Turning happened."

Of course, not everyone involved in this adventure calls it the Great Turning. You don't need that name in order to fight for survival and fashion a sane and decent future. For me, as a teacher, activist, and grandmother, the Great Turning helps me see what the physical eye cannot. It illumines more of the forces at play and the direction they are taking. At the same time, it sharpens my perception of the actual, concrete ways people are engaging in this global transformation. In other words, it serves as both compass and lens.

THE BIG PICTURE

From the countless social and environmental issues that compete for attention, we can take on isolated causes and support them with courage and devotion. But the forces we confront seem so great, and time so short, that it's easy to fear that our efforts are too scattered to be of real consequence. We tend to fall into the same short-term thinking that has entrapped our political economy.

The Great Turning invites us to lift our eyes from the cramped closet of short-term thinking and see the broader historical landscape. What a difference it makes to view our efforts as part of a vaster enterprise! Some social thinkers have already observed that this turning is comparable in magnitude to the Agricultural Revolution of the late Neolithic era, ten thousand years ago, and the Industrial Revolution of two-and-a-half centuries ago. The first one took centuries to unfold. The second only took generations. Right on its heels, as the industrial growth society spins out of control, comes this third revolution with diverse names such as "environmental revolution" or "ecological revolution" or "sustainability revolution." As is frequently noted, this transition must happen not in centuries or generations, but within a matter of years. That is because we have exceeded the limits of what the earth can restore and absorb. In systems terms, our economy is on *overshoot* and exponential *runaway*. This revolution must not only occur in a shorter time, it must also be more thorough, changing not only institutions and technologies but also the attitudes and habits that sustain them.

William Ruckelshaus, first director of the Environmental Protection Agency, from 1970 to 1973, reflected that while the first two revolutions "were gradual, spontaneous, and largely unconscious, this [third] one will have to be a fully conscious operation. If we actually do it, the undertaking will be absolutely unique in humanity's stay on Earth."[1]

As compass, the Great Turning helps us see the direction in which our political economy is headed. Because that economy is based on an impossible imperative—limitless increase in corporate profits—its trajectory leads to collapse. No system can endure that seeks to maximize a single variable. No possibility exists for unlimited growth in a finite planet. To quote Gus Speth, former head of the United Nations Development Program, "Our world, our only habitat, is a biotic system under such stress that it threatens to fail in fundamental and irreversible ways."[2]

Yet life is a dynamic process, self-organizing to adapt and evolve. Just as it turned scales into feathers, gills into lungs, and seawater into blood, so now, too, immense evolutionary forces are at work. They are driving this revolution of ours through innumerable, molecular, intersecting alterations in the human capacity for conscious change.

NO GUARANTEE

As Earth's record attests, extinctions are as plentiful as successful adaptations. We may not make it this time. Natural systems may unravel beyond repair before new sustainable forms and structures take hold. Many of us assumed that we could achieve a life-sustaining society without the collapse of the global corporate economy. But given the depth and breadth of the unraveling, breakdown now seems inevitable. Anguish over such widespread loss has touched all parts of the world.

That anguish is unavoidable if we stay honest and alert. The Great Turning comes with no guarantees. Its risk of failure is its reality. Insisting on belief in a positive outcome puts blinders on us and burdens the heart. We might manage to convince ourselves that everything will surely turn out all right, but would such reassurance elicit our greatest courage and creativity?

When you make peace with uncertainty, you find a kind of liberation. You are freed from bracing yourself against every piece of bad news and from constantly having to work up a sense of hopefulness in order to act. There is a certain equanimity and moral economy that comes when you are not constantly computing your chance of success. The enterprise is so vast that there is no way to judge the effects of this or that individual effort, or the extent to which it makes any difference at all. Once we acknowledge this, we can enjoy the challenge and the adventure. Then we can see that it is a privilege to be alive now in this Great Turning, when all the wisdom and courage ever harvested can be put to use.

There is no guarantee that this tremendous shift will kick in before our life support systems unravel irretrievably. From our own life experience, we know that there's never a guarantee—whether we're falling in love, going into labor to birth a baby, or devoting ourselves to a piece of land, turning the soil and watching for rain. We don't ask for proof that we'll succeed and that everything will turn out as we want. We just go ahead, because life wants to live through us.

THE THREE DIMENSIONS

The term the *Great Turning* is just one way to name the vast revolution that's going on because our way of life cannot be sustained. There are three main dimensions of it that I see: *Holding Actions, Structural Change,* and *Shift in Consciousness.*

The first dimension, *Holding Actions,* aims to slow the pace of destruction caused by the industrial growth society. This is important, because such actions buy time. They are like a first line of defense; they can save some species, some ecosystems, and some of the gene pool for future generations. Here we find what is generally called *activism.* It consists of all the political, legislative, legal, and regulatory work undertaken to slow down the destruction inflicted by the industrial growth society, but it also includes direct actions like blockades, boycotts, and civil disobedience. Although insufficient by themselves to bring about an alternative society, holding actions are necessary to the preservation of life. These actions hinder moves to give global corporations a free hand in plundering our heritage.

Over the last few years, we have seen incredible courage in people demanding human and environmental rights at Standing Rock, at the Keystone XL Pipeline, and at the Hambach Forest in Germany. The Sunrise Movement, Extinction Rebellion, and Earth Guardians are making it clear that climate action must be climate justice, with people of color and youth front and center.

Let's face it: this first dimension is exhausting. You can get stressed out of your mind by nonstop crises, the constant search for funding, the battles lost, and the increasing violence against activists. When you step back to take a breather, you often feel as if you are abandoning ship. But this is not the case. Don't be discouraged. Just keep on with the Great Turning in another form, the way the head goose, when she's tired, slips back and flies with the rest of the flock in the wind stream while another flyer takes her place.

Holding actions, after all, are not enough to create a sustainable society. In the second dimension, *Structural Change*, we learn to see how our current systems drive destructive behavior and how we can create alternative structures to replace them.

To free ourselves and our planet from the industrial growth society, we must understand its dynamics. What assumptions and structures lead us to use Earth as our supply house and sewer? What tacit agreements are creating obscene wealth for a few, while the great majority of humanity sinks into poverty and want? Not that long ago, it was hard slogging to raise public interest in the Intergovernmental Panel on Climate Change (IPCC); people's eyes glazed over. But now, as an upsurge of books, articles, teach-ins, and demonstrations demystifies the workings and impacts of the fossil fuel economy, we are wising up.

Clarity as to how the old system functions helps us see how and what to grow in its place. Alternative institutions and ways of doing things are proliferating, from local currencies to solar cooperatives, from ecovillages to community-supported agriculture. At no other epoch of human history have so many new ways of doing things appeared and in so short a time. Some may *look* marginal to us today, but they hold the seeds of the future. Today's actions bring together people across the spectrum, from labor unions to racial justice and environmental groups, increasingly making common cause.

Yet, as promising as they are, these forms and structures will shrivel and die unless they are rooted in deeply held values—in our sense of who we are, who we want to be, and how we relate to each other and the living body of Earth. To proliferate and endure, they must mirror a profound change in our perception of reality.

The third dimension of the Great Turning, *Shift in Consciousness*, is, at root, a spiritual revolution, awakening perceptions and values that are both new and ancient, flowing from rivers of ancestral wisdom. These values are expressed in songs, sermons, stories, and demonstrators' signs and banners, often with exuberance and humor.

This cognitive revolution is paralleled by a spiritual one. Ancient teachings speak to us now, showing us the beauty and power that can be ours as conscious, responsible members of the living body of Earth. Like our ancestors, we begin again to see the world as our larger body, and—whether we say the word or not—as *sacred*. This shift in our sense of identity will be lifesaving in the sociopolitical and ecological ordeals that lie before us.

Of course, a shift in consciousness by itself is insufficient for the Great Turning; you have to have holding actions and new structures as well. These three dimensions are totally interdependent and mutually reinforcing. I love seeing it this way because it gets us off that old argument: "Is it more important to work on yourself? Or is it more important to be out there on the barricades?" Those are such useless arguments, because actually we have to do it all. And as we do it together, the work gains momentum and becomes more self-sustaining.

Together, these three dimensions free us from the grip of the industrial growth society. They offer us nobler goals and truer pleasures. They preserve us from paralysis or panic when things get hard, helping us to resist the temptation to stick our heads in the sand or seek scapegoats for our fears. They help us move forward with trust in ourselves and each other, so that we can join hands in learning how the world self-heals and regenerates.

A new generation of organizers in the Buddhist Peace Fellowship expresses these three dimensions of the Great Turning in this handy formula: Block, Build, Be. Trainings, simply expressed as BBB, prepare us for "bold, creative, loving actions to *block* systemic harm, while *building* collaborative tools that help us *be* with our suffering in order to be free."

AUTHENTIC SPIRITUALITY

Everywhere I go, talking with people of all ages and walks of life, I sense this search for authenticity. People want to take responsibility for their lives, both politically and spiritually. They want to find a way through denial to deeper truth and human dignity. At the most fundamental level, there's an appetite for reconnecting with the sacred. Instead of depending on anyone else for that connection, we want to be able to know it and embody it ourselves.

What is the sacred? It is the ground of our being. It's the whole of which we are a part. It's what imbues our life with meaning and beauty. Of course, there are different ways of perceiving our relation to it. Mainstream Western society has, by and large, related to the sacred by projecting it outward, setting it apart as a God "out there" to worship and obey. We made the sacred transcendent, and in its honor, we created mosques, cathedrals, masterpieces of art and choral music—some of our greatest cultural achievements. But after several millennia of assigning the sacred to a transcendent dimension removed from ordinary life, the world around us began to go dead and lose its luminosity and meaning.

What is so beautiful about being alive at this moment is that the pendulum is starting to swing the other way. We are retrieving the projection. We are taking the sacred back into our lives. The swing is from transcendence to immanence. The most vital movement of our era involves making the sacred immanent again. I see it happening in every spiritual tradition—in the Jewish Renewal Movement, in Creation Spirituality, in women's spirituality, and in the teachings of indigenous peoples. We are reawakening to the sacredness of life itself, in the soil and air and water, in our brothers and sisters of other species, and in our own bodies.

I spoke of this as a swing of the pendulum, but a metaphor I like even better comes from Ludwig Feuerbach, a German theologian of the mid-nineteenth century. He said that our apprehensions of the sacred have a rhythm like the pumping action of the heart.[3] Just as the heart pumps blood out from the center of the body, we project outward our sense of the sacred, so that we can behold its majesty and fall on our knees before it in wonder and awe. But Feuerbach reminded us that the heartbeat is a two-way action: the pumping out is followed by the drawing blood back into the heart. When the sacred becomes too remote, you take it back in to let it vitalize your life. The retrieval of the projection is not an endpoint either. When we get stuck too long in immanence, the sacred becomes indistinguishable from anything else; it becomes bland, taken for granted. So, the heartbeat goes on, ever renewing our sense of the holy. To perceive it this way frees us to see that these two movements of the heart need each other.

To see all life as holy rescues us from loneliness and the sense of futility that comes with isolation. The sacred becomes part of every encounter when you open to it and let it receive your full attention. I don't have to go to Chartres Cathedral to be in the presence of the Divine. It is right here. This understanding is essential for facing collapse and living in this time.

This means that our sorrow is sacred, too. Within us, all is grief for what is happening to our world—the despoiling of earth, the extinction of our brother and sister species, the massive suffering of our fellow humans, the terrible injustice of dominated and colonized peoples. But when we feel isolated, we stifle that sorrow and rage in order to fit in better and to avoid aggravating the loneliness.

Experiencing the sacred as immanent helps people to befriend their pain for the world and not fear that it will isolate them. Moral distress is not only honored in all spiritual traditions, it also serves as wholesome feedback, necessary for our survival. To recognize this brings us back to life: It's okay for me to be here. It's okay for me to weep for the horrors that have befallen people of color and all those oppressed and brutalized. It's okay for me to weep for generations who aren't even born yet. That's because *I belong*. That's because *I am part of the sacred living body of Earth.*

When you act on behalf of something greater than yourself, you begin to feel it acting through you with a power that is greater than your own. The religious term for this empowerment is *grace*, and grace has been primarily conceived as coming from God. But now we are feeling graced by other beings and by Earth itself. Those with whom and on whose behalf we act give us strength and eloquence, a staying power we didn't know we had.

THE WAY AHEAD

In these recent years, I sometimes meet people with a sense of recognition that they are *children of the passage*. And this passage, I sense, is toward a planetary culture. They will have a hard time surviving the collapse, and the passage will probably take generations. But it is arrogant to assume we can know that this time of ours will be the end of complex life forms.

For my whole life, I have loved finding ways that give people the skills and motivation to work together. We have been so atomized by the hyper-individualism of the last five centuries that we've become a bit passive, scared, and obedient. Now is such a sweetly powerful time to meet and learn to trust in what I call "rough weather networks." These will help us find each other and develop strong habits of the heart, as well as some good stone soup recipes.

Sometimes I'm asked, "Where is the Great Turning? Everything is falling apart." The Great Turning is not an alternative to collapse; it is the vision and commitment that will bond us and move us *through* collapse. The breakdown of global corporate capitalism will be messier than we can imagine. There's going to be a lot of dying and losses of all kinds. Yet, right in the midst of it, we will wake up, be taken out of our small selves, and washed clean by the power of our allegiance to life. What stories will we take with us? What songs will release our laughter and love?

The Great Turning helps me turn toward what is possible and allows me to live with an open heart. It causes me to believe that whether we succeed or not, the risks we take on behalf of life will bring forth dimensions of human intelligence and solidarity beyond any we have known.

SIXTEEN

COLLECTIVE INTELLIGENCE: THE HOLONIC SHIFT

Let me fall if I must fall.
The one I am becoming
will catch me.

—BAAL SHEM TOV

A shift in consciousness toward the collective is critical for the Great Turning and even our survival. We are getting inklings of it right now in shared perceptions of common dangers and in experiences of synergy as we face these dangers creatively. We are tuning to each other more, our antennae are picking up more signals, and the internet is accelerating the process. One way that this is becoming evident is in the growing number of experiences people are having that don't fit with their ordinary, ego-identified mentality. When people become conscious of radically new insights, they sometimes imagine them to be coming "from outside"—through clairvoyance or telepathy or channeling. But instead of interventions from a supernatural dimension, these "messages" more likely reflect the gradual emergence of a wider level of consciousness arising from our own systemic interactions. We are like neurons in a larger brain, and we are becoming aware that that larger brain is thinking.

Given the depletion and fragility of life on our planet, and given our need for creative flexibility and sharing, we need to think *together* in an integrated, synergistic fashion, rather than in the old fragmented and competitive ways.

For most of us, until now, intelligence has been seen as a function of separate brains lodged inside separate skulls. But now our interactions—the massive ways we impinge on each other economically, politically, and militarily—are becoming so complex and interlocked that a built-in self-monitoring capacity becomes necessary. This may involve artificial intelligence, but it *requires* human intelligence, judgment, and moral choice-making.

As open systems dependent upon larger, evolving systems, we must stay open to the wider flows of information, no matter how painful they are or how inimical they appear to our primitive notions of self-interest. What is required of us, for our survival, is an expanded sense of self-interest, one in which the needs of the whole—and the other beings within that whole—are seen as commensurate with our own. Only then can we begin to think and act together. For that we need what Buddhists call a "boundless heart," and I believe we have that boundless heart within us by virtue of our nature as open systems.

Whether sub-organic like a molecule, organic like a cell or human body, or supra-organic like a society or ecosystem, all living systems can be seen as *holons*. That means they have a dual nature: they are both wholes in themselves and, simultaneously, integral parts of larger wholes. Writer and systems thinker Arthur Koestler coined the term *holon* from the Greek word for "whole," plus the suffix *on*, meaning "part."[1]

Living phenomena, therefore, appear as systems within systems, fields within fields, like a set of Chinese boxes or Russian dolls. Each represents a level of organization provided by the interactions of systems at the previous level. The interactions of atoms provide the organizational basis for molecules, and those of molecules for cells, and cells for organs and organisms, and organisms for communities, and so forth. Life is organized into nested hierarchies. Since they are not characterized by any top-down chain of command, a condition associated with the term *hierarchy*, some theorists prefer to say *holonarchy*.

THE MYSTERY OF EMERGENCE

In this step-wise organization of living systems, *emergence* is a universal and striking feature. At each holonic level, new properties and new possibilities emerge that could not have been predicted. From the respective qualities of oxygen and hydrogen, for example, you would never guess the properties that emerge when they interact to make water. Or take steel—the synergistic strength of iron and nickel combined far exceeds the strength of one added to the strength of the other.

From the systems perspective, mind or consciousness arises even in rudimentary form by virtue of feedback loops that permit even the simplest living systems to self-correct, adapt, and evolve. Self-reflexive consciousness, however, seems to emerge at the level of some large-brained animals, like humans. Here the system's internal complexity has become so great that it can no longer meet its needs by trial and error. It needs to evolve another level of awareness in order to weigh competing courses of action; it needs, in other words, to be able to make choices. The "I" appears. The necessity of making decisions brings about self-reflexivity.

Self-reflexive consciousness does *not*, however, characterize the next holonic level, the level of social systems. In tight-knit organizations with strong allegiances, one can sense an "esprit de corps," or group mind, but this mentality is still too weak and too undifferentiated for active response on its own behalf. The locus of decision-making remains within the individual, susceptible to all the vagaries of what that individual considers to be of "self-interest." And our present modes of collective decision-making are simply too slow and too corruptible to respond adequately to the survival crises produced by the industrial growth society and its technologies. But could these very crises, confronting us with the destruction of complex life forms on Earth, engender a collective level of self-interest in choice making? That would be, in other words, self-reflexivity on the next holonic level, or a *holonic shift*.

Fearful of fascism, we might well want to reject any idea of collective consciousness. It is important, therefore, to remember that an open system requires diversity of parts, and the greater the variety, the more cybernetically stable and adaptive it is. A monolith of uniformity has no internal intelligence. As political scientist and systems thinker Karl Deutsch has pointed out, healthy social systems require a plurality of views and free circulation of information. The holonic shift does not sacrifice, but rather *requires*, the uniqueness of each part and of its point of view.

It begins, almost imperceptibly, with a sense of common fate and a shared intention to meet it together. It starts to emerge in unexpected behaviors, as individuals in countless settings meet to speak and reflect on what is happening to their lives, their world. It manifests in an unpredictable array of spontaneous actions, as people step out from their private comforts, giving time and taking risks on behalf of life on Earth. It includes all the behavioral changes that bring forth the Great Turning. And given the dynamics of self-organizing systems, it is likely that as we reflect and act together, we will soon find ourselves responding to the present crisis with far greater confidence and precision than we imagined possible.

OUR COLLECTIVE PURPOSE

Whether or not we choose to explain it in terms of systems theory, the holonic shift can serve as a metaphor for our collective purpose and for our emerging sense of identity as a planet people. How can we as individuals promote and take part in it? Here are some guidelines we drew up at the end of a week-long intensive in Germany in 1994, as we felt the thrill of collective intelligence becoming a reality.

1. *Attune to a common intention.* This intention is not a goal or plan that you can formulate with precision. It is rather an open-ended aim: that we may work together to meet common needs and collaborate in new ways.

2. *Welcome diversity.* Self-organization of the whole requires differentiation of the parts. Each one's role in this unfolding journey is unique and valuable.

3. *Know that only the whole can repair itself.* We cannot "fix" the world, but we can take part in its self-healing. Healing wounded relationships and legacies is integral to the healing of our world.

4. *Learn to trust.* You are only a small part of a much larger process, like a nerve cell in a neural net. Trust means taking part and taking risks when you cannot control or even know the outcome.

5. *Open to flows of information from the larger system.* Do not resist painful information about the condition of our world. Understand that your suffering for the world arises from connection and unblocks feedback necessary for the well-being of the whole.

6. *Speak the truth of your experience of this world.* If you have persistent responses to present conditions, assume that they are shared by others. Willing to drop old answers and old roles, give voice to the questions arising in you.

7. *Believe no one who claims to have the final answer.* Such claims are a sign of ignorance and limited self-interest.

8. *Work in teams on joint projects serving common intentions.* Build community through shared tasks and rituals.

9. *Be generous with your strengths and skills.* They are not your private property, and they grow from being shared. They include both your knowing and your not knowing, as well as the gifts you accept from the ancestors and all beings.

10. *Draw forth the strengths of others.* Acknowledge and appreciate their strengths. Never pre-judge what a person can contribute, but be ready for surprises and fresh forms of synergy.

11. *Be content with not seeing the results of your work.* Your actions may have unanticipated and far-reaching effects unknown to you in your lifetime.

12. *Let there be serenity in all your doing.* Even while putting forth great effort, you are held within the web of life, within flows of energy and intelligence far exceeding your own.

This journey that is the holonic shift can be experienced more richly now because of the diversity and complexity of this historical moment. And what an amazing moment it is, when we have the capacity to destroy all life on earth and also the capacity to choose a new flowering of life. We can recognize our commonality with fresh tenderness and come home to our mutual belonging.

SEVENTEEN

SHAMBHALA WARRIORS:
A PROPHECY

I want to be famous in a way a pulley is famous,
or a buttonhole, not because it did anything spectacular,
but because it never forgot what it could do.

—NAOMI SHIHAB NYE

In 1980, while visiting Tibetan friends living in exile in India, I learned of a prophecy that had arisen in their Buddhist tradition over twelve centuries ago. Known as the coming of the kingdom of Shambhala, it foretold, they said, dire dangers not unlike those of our present planet-time.

There are varying interpretations of this prophecy. Some portray the coming of the kingdom of Shambhala as an internal event, a metaphor for one's inner spiritual journey, independent of the world around us. Others present it as an entirely external event that will unfold in our world regardless of what we choose to do. The third understanding of the prophecy, featuring the interplay between self and world, is the one given to me by my friend and teacher Dugu Choegyal Rinpoche of the Tashi Jong community in northern India. It has entered and influenced my life, and I have shared it over the years as I heard it with people studying with me.

THE PROPHECY

There comes a time when all life on Earth is in danger. In this time, great barbarian powers have arisen. Although these powers spend their wealth in preparations to annihilate each other, they have much in common: weapons of unfathomable devastation and death, and technologies that lay waste our world. It is in this time, when the future of sentient life hangs by the frailest of threads, that the kingdom of Shambhala emerges.

You can't go there, for it is not a geographic place. It exists in the hearts and minds of the Shambhala warriors. Now, you cannot recognize Shambhala warriors by sight, for they wear no uniform or insignia. They have no flags or banners, no barricades on which to threaten the enemy or behind which they can rest and regroup. They don't even have any home turf. Always they must move across the very terrain of the barbarians.

Now the time comes when great courage is required of the Shambhala warriors—moral courage and physical courage, for they must go into the heart of the barbarian power. They must go to the pits and citadels where the weapons are kept in order to dismantle them. To dismantle the weapons, in every sense of the word, they must go into the corridors of power where decisions are made.

The Shambhala warriors know they can do this, because these weapons are *manomaya*, "mind-made." Made by the human mind, they can be unmade by the human mind. The Shambhala warriors know the dangers that threaten life on Earth are not visited upon us by any extraterrestrial powers, satanic deities, or preordained evil fate. They arise from our own choices, our priorities and relationships.

So, in this time, the Shambhala warriors go into training. When Choegyal Rinpoche said this, I asked, "How do they train?" They train, he said, in the use of two weapons. "What weapons?" I asked, and he held up his hands in the way the lamas hold the ritual objects of bell and *dorje* in the great monastic dances of his people.

The weapons are compassion and insight. Both are necessary, he said. You have to have compassion, because it gives you the fuel to move you out there, to do what is needed. It essentially means not being afraid of the suffering of your world. But this weapon is very hot. It can burn you out, so you need the other weapon—you need insight into the radical interdependence of all phenomena. With that wisdom, you know it is not a battle between good guys and bad guys, for the line between good and evil runs through the landscape of every human heart. We are so profoundly interwoven that actions undertaken with pure intent have repercussions throughout the web of life, beyond your capacity to measure or discern. By itself, that insight may appear too cool, too conceptual, to sustain you and keep you moving, so you need the heat of the compassion, the openness to the world's pain.

Together, within each Shambhala warrior and among the warriors themselves, these two can sustain us in our work. They are gifts we can claim now for the healing of our world.

AFTERTHOUGHT

On that unforgettable day when I heard my friend recount the prophecy, I ran down the hill to where my family was staying and shared the prophecy with them. As I finished that first telling, my son Jack looked puzzled. "But Mom, didn't he say how it was all going to turn out?" I laughed and said, "If Choegyal Rinpoche had told me how it was going to turn out, I wouldn't have believed *any* of it. And don't you believe anyone who tells you they know what's in store for us."

After I began offering workshops, I occasionally included a telling of the Shambhala Prophecy. As I saw the impact on the listeners, I shared the prophecy more often, though I still had never written it down, knowing that it belonged to an oral tradition. It was when I learned that some people had published in their own books what they heard me say that I decided to put it in writing myself, in the words I recalled from the start.

Over the years, I've realized that one of the most useful insights for people today is the exchange I had with Jack. I emphasize the importance of *not knowing* the outcome, because the desire for certainty can distract our attention and warp our perceptions. Liberated from the need for certainty—and even hope—we can more fully inhabit the present moment. Not knowing rivets our attention on what is happening right now. This present moment is the only time we can act, and the only time, after all, we can wake up.

EIGHTEEN

COURAGE FOR THE ROAD

*Sometimes it is the artist's task to find out
how much music you can still make
with what you have left.*

—ITZHAK PERLMAN

After I gave the first public workshop in 1980 that set the ball rolling for the Work That Reconnects, a seasoned activist asked me, "Why are you doing this?" Well, I *thought* I was doing it to help us all be more effective at social change. But when I answered, the words came right from my solar plexus, "I'm doing it so that when things fall apart, we will not turn on each other."

Now, four decades later, that may be the biggest challenge. The powers that have gained political traction know quite well how to manipulate a nation's fears and weaknesses. When people are ravaged by an ever-surging pandemic at the same time that they watch their jobs disappear and the economy crumble, their helpless rage makes them easy targets. With the Amazon and the Arctic aflame, the boreal forests burning, old resentments can be quickly ignited. For even climate change deniers are, like the rest of us, part of Earth's living body, though embrittled perhaps by their refusal to acknowledge it.

After Donald Trump's election, some forty of us met at Ghost Ranch in the Sangre de Cristo Mountains of New Mexico over his inauguration week for reflection and grounding. We called our gathering "In the Dark, the Eye Learns to See," words from a Theodore Roethke poem. The electoral campaign we had just lived through had revealed the power of lies to distort people's perceptions and turn a nation against itself. We wondered together: How do we face the dangers of this time and learn to see each other with a measure of trust? What does the threat of fascism demand of us? How do we work for solidarity and communication across the many divides in our culture?

Erica Peng, a colleague teaching at the Haas School of Business at UC Berkeley, was with us that week. Her class on Embodied Leadership draws on both neuroscience and the Work That Reconnects. At Ghost Ranch she led us in exercises to facilitate communication with people across strong disagreement. These allowed us to shift to emotional states that don't raise our blood pressure, but instead help open the way to receptivity. When we tried shifting our attitude toward the other person from *contempt* to *curiosity*, the change we experienced in mood and ease of communication was dramatic. The contrast was so marked that we felt liberated into new possibilities of connection with those we consider "difficult." The same, we found, is true of fear: curiosity is the way to step out of it.

None of us back then in 2017 could have imagined the polarization that four years under the forty-fifth president of the United States would bring us. Never could I have guessed that so many citizens work so hard for so long to make sure that a president didn't have another four years in office. Though he lost by seven million votes, he refused to accept defeat, maintaining that he was

the actual winner, and inflaming supporters with his determination to stay on as their president. Defending this claim of victory,
his followers staged the first-ever violent domestic assault on the
US Capitol, adding to the entrenched polarization in Congress and
in the country. Since that insurrection, Democratic legislators face
daily threats of violence from elected extremist Republicans who
have gone so far as to smuggle guns into Congress.

The polarization that we face today is far more serious than
what we sensed four years ago, and the need to deal with it
more urgent. The future of life depends on it. Why? Because
for the sake of that future our greenhouse gas emissions must
be reduced right away, and that requires the self-reflexive consciousness we embody as human beings. We must act *together*
and we can't do that if we're at each other's throats. We've got
to find ways to trust each other.

I take heart when I think about the Shambhala warriors.
They are less vulnerable to dissention, thanks to their "weapons" of compassion and wisdom. They are open to the suffering
of others and realize that the line between good and evil runs
through every human heart. They are not tempted to demonize
others and see them as evil.

So how do we learn to connect with each other when we
don't agree at all? People are already practicing skills for communicating across the chasms that divide us. Organizations like
Braver Angels and the Purple Path offer creative methods that
invite the expression of raw honesty while helping people cultivate respect for each other's sincerity.

With trust, we might begin to feel, *Here is a brother or sister,
brought by the intelligence of Earth to be alive at this moment.*
This person might also have a sense that life needs to go on and

that they have something to contribute. Then we have something in common. Instead of judgment, contempt or blame, the conversation shifts, bringing energy and caring.

Such work is even more essential now, because since 2020 our general consensus reality, our shared mental world, has been shattered, says Richard Heinberg, founder of the Post Carbon Institute and a teacher to me for decades. Areas where we can agree have been blown out the window. He explains how the internet and social media have a disintegrating effect on our connectivity as a culture and a country. "Algorithms capture users' interests and prejudices and feed them news and opinion articles that lead them to ever more extreme views."

When the very media we employ to inform ourselves and communicate with others exaggerates our differences and grievances, fractures in our common culture begin not to heal, but to widen. "Individuals find themselves not just disagreeing on politics or religion, but living in different and directly conflicting mental universes," says Heinberg. The collective risks of consensus breakdown include widespread rage and murderous impulses.

"The brain on grievance craves retribution," says brain researcher James Kimmel Jr. of Yale University. "Consensus breakdown can contribute to a self-reinforcing process of collapse." One of its effects is the lowering of social trust. Trust, after all, is the basis of cooperation, and high levels of cooperation are required for modern complex societies to function.

Some reports indicate that more than a third of Americans are so alienated that they prefer to believe obviously fabricated lies whose accuracy is dubious. This is because they are emotionally confirming for people who refuse to accept the dominant narrative. The goal of wrecking the consensus becomes more important than democracy itself. This has grave implications for the support and credibility the new US head of state needs to be able to count on in order to govern effectively.

From the perspective of the Great Turning, the rage is understandable. The Buddha said you can't meditate on an empty stomach; you have to have a social program with right livelihood, sharing, and sufficiency for all. And we know now that this Turning, when it's actually unfolding, involves three mutually supportive understandings. First, we are sacred, as is our Earth, and we can rise up from the ashes as a planet people. Second, that we can slow down and not cooperate with the corporate-driven economy that wrecks our Earth and empties our lives. And third, that we already have what it takes—in energy, skills, and collaborative capacity—to build the foundations for a life-sustaining economy and culture.

We find our dignity and purpose in the Great Turning, as scales fall from our eyes and we see that transforming Nature into money doesn't work. We discover that a deep ecological vision can bring us through with all that we are and can become. We are cleansed by the truth of belonging to Earth. And in this very act we allow ourselves to recognize that we may not be able to avoid the collapse of our planet as a home for life that has evolved over millions of years. In either case, we move forth as a human family, as a planet people bearing the gifts and injuries of our Ancestors, right along with all other life forms on this planet.

The Spiral emerged as the throughline in the Work That Reconnects with the many practices it offers. The largest US-based facilitator development program is now called The Spiral Journey. For many of us in recent years, the Spiral has surfaced as a practice in itself, like a fractal or a distillation of the Work that brings us energy, renewal, and fresh perspective. Even in moments, in a glancing thought when we are shaken, we can turn to the Spiral. And now, as we leave these pages, we can take it with us on the road.

First, let us ground ourselves in gratitude. To effect any real change, gladness to be here is essential. We have shown up at possibly the most critical and challenging moment for life on earth. We have come with self-reflexive consciousness, so we have the power to choose. And as humans, furthermore, we can speak and be heard by other humans in our communities and at the highest levels of power. For the sake of solidarity with the rest of humanity, we can resolve or transcend our quarrels and awaken as a Planet People.

Second, we can befriend our world. Instead of denying or numbing the pain we feel for its suffering, we can honor it. We need not fear the anguish that comes; it is not a weakness or illness. That heartbreak is a measure of both our belonging and our caring. These are doorways to the healing we bring when we come together as a Planet People.

We are able to see with new eyes when we shift to a new perspective. This experience is fueled and informed by discovering that our world is both our lover and our self. We learn to trust our commonality with people from all walks of life and through all periods of time. As this happens, we begin to see ourselves and one another as a Planet People, or on the fast track to becoming so, ready or not.

Empty of everything but the present moment and the practice itself, we are free to go forth into uncertainty, for now is the only time we can act, the only time to wake up. There is no need to compete or win out over others. A deeper ache, a more ancient desire, takes hold and with it, a broader field for the choices we make. It is time to go forth for the sake of the living planet we now realize ourselves to be. In fulfillment of the invitation the Buddha offered two and a half millennia ago, let us go forth for the welfare and happiness of all beings.

Go forth on your journey, for the benefit of the many,

For the joy of the many, out of compassion for the welfare,

The benefit and joy of all beings.

SPIRITUAL PRACTICES
FOR ACTIVISTS

· *You and I are flowers of a tenacious family.*
Breathe slowly and deeply,
Free of previous occupation.
The latest good news
Is that you can do it,
And that I can take time to do it too, with you.

—MARCI THURSTON SHAINE

To heal our society, our psyches must heal as well. Haunted by the desperate needs of our time and beset by more commitments than we can easily carry, we may wonder how to find the time and energy for spiritual disciplines.

Yet we do not need to withdraw from the world or spend long hours in solitary prayer or meditation to begin to wake up to the contemplative capacity within us. The activities and encounters of our daily lives can serve as the occasion for that kind of discovery. I would like to share eight simple practices that can help in this.

The practices—on lovingkindness, death, compassion, mutual power, and mutual recognition—are adapted from the Buddhist tradition. As part of our planetary heritage, they belong to us all. No belief system is necessary, only a readiness to attend

to the immediacy of our own experience. They will be most useful
if read slowly with a quiet mind (a few deep breaths will help)
and if put directly into practice as you go about your day. If you
read them aloud for others or record them for yourself, allow several seconds of breath and pause throughout. In a group setting,
the words in italics are to be spoken by the guide or facilitator.

1. MEDITATION ON LOVINGKINDNESS

On the Buddhist path, lovingkindness, or metta, is the first of
the Four Immeasurables, also known as the Brahmaviharas. It
is a meditation to arouse and sustain lovingkindness. When I
worked with the Buddhist-inspired community development
movement in Sri Lanka, I was struck by the near constant use
of metta practice. Until then, I thought it was reserved for the
meditation cushion, but now I saw it evoked in the heat and
sweat of village work. Organizers and village workers used
metta to arouse villager motivation for service and overcome
feelings of inadequacy in themselves and others.

I first received instruction in this meditation from a nun
in the Tibetan Buddhist tradition. Here is a version that I have
adapted for use in the West.

Close your eyes and begin to relax, exhaling to expel tension.
Now center in on the normal flow of the breath, letting go of
all extraneous thoughts as you passively watch the breathing-in
and breathing-out. . . .

Now call to mind someone you love very dearly. . . . In your
mind's eye, see the face of that beloved one. . . . Silently speak
their name. . . . Feel your love for this being, like a current of

energy coming through you. . . . Now let yourself experience how much you want this person to be free from fear, how intensely you desire that this person be released from greed and ill will, from confusion and sorrow and the causes of suffering. . . . That desire, in all its sincerity and strength, is metta, the great loving-kindness. . . .

Continuing to feel that warm current of energy coming through the heart, see in your mind's eye those with whom you share your daily life: family members, close friends and colleagues, the people you live and work with. . . . Let them appear now as in a circle around you. Behold them one by one, and direct to each, in turn, that same current of lovingkindness. . . . Among these beings may be some with whom you are uncomfortable, in conflict or tension. With those especially, experience your desire that each be free from fear, from hatred, free from greed, ignorance, and the causes of suffering. . . .

Now allow to appear, in wider concentric circles, your relations and your acquaintances. . . . Let the beam of lovingkindness play on them as well, pausing on the faces that appear randomly in your mind's eye. With them as well, experience how much you want their freedom from greed, fear, hatred, and confusion, how much you want all beings to be happy. . . .

Beyond them, in concentric circles that are wider yet, appear now all beings with whom you share this planet-time. Though you have not met, your lives are interconnected in ways beyond knowing. To these beings as well, direct the same powerful current of lovingkindness. . . . Experience your desire and your intention that each awaken from fear and hatred, from greed and confusion . . . that all beings be released from suffering. . . .

As in the ancient Buddhist meditation, we direct the loving-kindness now to all the hungry ghosts, the restless spirits that are still prey to fear and confusion. May they find rest . . . may they rest in the great lovingkindness and in the deep peace it brings. . . .

By the power of our imagination, let us move out now beyond our planet, out into the universe, into other solar systems, other galaxies, other Buddha fields. The current of lovingkindness is not diminished by physical distances, and we direct it now, as if aiming a beam of light, to all conscious life. . . . To all beings everywhere, we direct our heartfelt wish that they, too, be free of fear and greed, of hatred and confusion and the causes of suffering. . . . May all beings be happy. . . .

Now, from out there in the interstellar distances, we turn and behold our own planet, our home. We see it suspended there in the blackness of space, a blue and white jewel planet turning in the light of its sun. Slowly we approach it, drawing nearer, nearer, returning to this region of it, this very place. . . . And as you approach this place, let yourself see the being you know best of all . . . the person it has been given you to be in this lifetime. . . . You know this person better than anyone else does, know its pain and its hopes, know its need and capacity for love, know how hard it tries. . . . Let the face of this being, your own face, appear before you. . . . Speak the name you are called in love. . . . And experience, with that same strong energy-current of lovingkindness, how deeply you desire that this being be free from fear and aversion . . . released from greed and delusion, . . . and liberated from competition and comparing mind. . . . The great lovingkindness linking you to all beings is now directed to your own self as well. . . . Know now the fullness of it.

2. MEDITATION ON DEATH

Most spiritual paths ask us to confront the transiency of human life. Medieval Christians honored this in the mystery play of *Everyman*. Don Juan, the Yaqui sorcerer, taught that the enlightened warrior walks with death at his shoulder. To confront and accept the inevitability of our dying releases us from attachments and frees us to live boldly.

An initial meditation on the Buddhist path involves reflection on the twofold fact that: *death is certain* and *the time of death is uncertain*. The massive dangers overshadowing our world today, including nuclear warheads still targeted and "on alert," serve that meditation, for they tell us we can die together at any moment, without warning. When we allow that possibility to become conscious, it is painful, but it also jolts us awake to life's vividness, its miraculous quality, heightening our awareness of the beauty and uniqueness of each object and each being. As an occasional practice in daily life:

> *Look at a person you encounter in everyday life, stranger or friend, perhaps someone on a bus or elevator or truck beside you in traffic. This person lives on an endangered planet. They may die in a nuclear war or from the poisons spreading through our world. Observe that face: unique, vulnerable. . . . Note that body, still whole and active. . . . Become aware of your desire that this person be spared such suffering and horror; feel the strength of that desire. . . . Keep breathing. . . . Imagine the possibility that this could be the person you happen to be with when you die . . . that face the last you see . . . that hand the last you touch. . . . It might reach out to help you then, to comfort, to give water. . . . Open to the feelings that surface in you with the awareness of this possibility. . . .*

3. BREATHING THROUGH

Basic to most spiritual traditions, as well as to the systems view of the world, is the recognition that we are not separate, isolated entities, but integral parts of the vast web of life. As such, we are like neurons in a neural net through which flow currents of awareness of what is happening to us as a species and as a planet. In that context, the pain we feel for our world is a living testimony to our interdependence. If we deny this pain, we become like blocked and atrophied neurons weakening the larger body in which we take being. But if we let it move through us, we affirm our belonging and our collective awareness increases. We can open to the pain of the world in confidence that it can neither shatter nor isolate us, for we are not objects that can break. We are resilient patterns within a vast web of knowing.

Because we have been conditioned to view ourselves as separate, competitive, and thus fragile entities, it takes practice to relearn this kind of resilience. A good way to begin is by practicing simple openness, as in the exercise of "breathing through," adapted from an ancient Buddhist meditation for the development of compassion. (This meditation is similar to *tonglen* practice, which also involves breathing in pain and suffering, but it is different in that it does not seek to transform that pain into healing before breathing it out.)

> *Closing your eyes, focus attention on your breathing. Don't try to breathe any special way, slow or long, just watch the breathing as it happens . . . in and out. . . . Note the sensations at the nostrils or upper lip, in the chest or abdomen. Stay passive and alert. . . .*

As you watch the breath, note that it happens by itself, without your will, without your deciding each time to inhale or exhale. . . . It's as though you're being breathed—being breathed by life. . . . Just as everyone in this room, in this city, in this planet now, is being breathed, sustained in a vast, breathing web of life. . . .

Now visualize your breath as a stream or ribbon of air passing through you. See it flow up through your nose, down through your windpipe, and into your lungs. Now from your lungs take it through your heart. . . . Picture it flowing through your heart and out through an opening there to reconnect with the larger web of life. Let the breath-stream, as it passes through you, appear as one loop within that vast web, connecting you with it. . . .

Now open your awareness to the suffering that is present in the world. For now, drop all defenses, and open to your knowledge of that suffering. Let it come as concretely as you can . . . in images of your fellow beings in prisons, hospitals, slums, refugee camps, scenes of war. . . . No need to strain for these images; they are present in you by virtue of our mutual belonging. Relax and just let them surface . . . the vast and countless hardships of our fellow humans . . . and of our animal brothers and sisters as well, as they swim the seas and fly the air of this ailing planet. . . . Now breathe in the pain like granules on the stream of air, up through your nose, down through your trachea, lungs, and heart, and out again into the web of life. . . . You are asked to do nothing for now, but let it pass through your heart. . . . Be sure that stream flows through and out again; don't hang on to the pain. . . . Surrender it for now to the healing resources of life's vast web. . . .

With Shantideva, the Buddhist saint, we can say, "Let all sorrows ripen in me." We help them ripen by passing them through our hearts . . . making good rich compost out of all that grief . . . so we can learn from it, enhancing our larger, collective knowing. . . .

If no images or feelings arise and there is only blankness, grey and numb, breathe that through. The numbness itself is a very real part of our world. . . .

And if what surfaces for you is not the pain of other beings so much as your own personal suffering, breathe that through, too. Your own anguish is an inextricable part of the grief of our world, and arises with it. . . .

Should you feel an ache in the chest, a pressure in the rib cage, as if the heart would break, that is all right. Your heart is not an object that can break. . . . But if it were, they say the heart that breaks open can hold the whole universe. Your heart is that large. . . . Trust it. Keep breathing. . . .

This guided meditation serves to introduce the process of breathing through, which, once familiar, becomes useful in daily life in the many situations that confront us with suffering. By breathing through the bad news, rather than bracing ourselves against it, we can let it strengthen our sense of belonging in the larger web of being. It helps us remain alert and open, whether reading the newspaper, receiving criticism, or simply being present to a person in pain.

For activists working for peace and justice, and for those dealing firsthand with the griefs of our time, the practice helps prevent burnout. Reminding us of the collective nature of both our problems and our power, it offers a healing measure of humility. It can save us from self-righteousness. For when we can take in our world's pain, accepting it as the price of our caring, we let it inform our acts without needing to inflict it as a punishment on others who seem less involved.

4. THE GREAT BALL OF MERIT

Compassion, which is grief in the grief of others, is but one side of the coin. The other side is joy in the joy of others—which in Buddhism is called *mudita*. To the extent that we allow ourselves to identify with the sufferings of other beings, we are able to identify with their strengths as well. This is very important for a sense of adequacy and resilience, because we face a time of great challenge that demands of us more commitment, endurance, and courage than we can dredge up out of our individual supply. We can learn to draw on the other neurons in the neural net and view them in a grateful and celebratory fashion, as so much "savings in the bank."

This practice is adapted from the *Meditation of Jubilation and Transformation*, taught in a Buddhist text written two thousand years ago at the outset of the Mahayana tradition. You can find the original version in chapter six of the *Perfection of Wisdom in 8,000 Lines*. I find it useful today in two forms. The one closer to the ancient practice is this:

> *Relax and close your eyes. Open your awareness to the fellow beings who share with you this planet-time . . . in this town . . . in this country . . . and in other lands. . . . See their multitudes in your mind's eye. . . . Now let your awareness open wider yet, to encompass all beings who ever lived . . . of all races and*

*creeds and walks of life, rich, poor, kings and beggars, saints
and sinners. . . . See the vast vistas of these fellow beings stretch-
ing into the distance, like successive mountain ranges. . . . You
know that in each of these innumerable lives some act of merit
was performed. No matter how stunted or deprived the life,
there was a gesture of generosity, a gift of love, an act of valor
or self-sacrifice . . . on the battlefield or workplace, hospital or
home. . . . From these beings in their endless multitudes arose
actions of courage and kindness, of teaching and healing. Let
yourself see these manifold and immeasurable acts of merit. . . .*

*Now imagine you can sweep together these acts of merit. . . .
Sweep them into a pile in front of you . . . .use your hands . . .
pile them up . . . pile them into a heap, beholding it with
gladness and gratitude. . . . Now form them into a ball. It is
the Great Ball of Merit. . . . Hold it now and weigh it in your
hands . . . rejoice in it, knowing that no act of goodness is ever
lost. It remains ever and always a present resource . . . a means
for the transformation of life. . . . So now, with jubilation and
gratitude, you turn that great ball . . . turn it over . . . and
over . . . into the healing of our world.*

As we can learn from contemporary science and visualize
in the holographic model of reality, our lives interpenetrate. In
the fluid tapestry of space-time, there is at root no distinction
between self and other. The acts and intentions of others are
like seeds that can germinate and bear fruit through our own
lives, as we take them into awareness and dedicate, or turn over
that awareness to our own empowerment. Thoreau, Gandhi,
Martin Luther King, Dorothy Day, Sojourner Truth, and countless nameless heroes and heroines of our own day, all can be

part of our Ball of Merit, from which we can draw inspiration and endurance. Other traditions feature notions similar to this, such as the "cloud of witnesses" spoken of in Paul's letters and the Treasury of Merit in the Catholic Church.

The second, more workaday version of the Ball of Merit meditation helps us open to the powers in people around us. It is in direct contrast to the commonly accepted patriarchal notion of power as something personally owned and exerted over others. The practice prepares us to bring expectant attention to our encounters with other beings, to view them with fresh openness and curiosity as to how they can enhance our Ball of Merit. We can play this inner game with someone near us on the train or across the bargaining table. It is especially useful when dealing with a person with whom we may be in conflict.

What does this person add to my Great Ball of Merit? What gifts of intellect can enrich our common store? What reserves of stubborn endurance can they offer? What flights of fancy or powers of love lurk behind those eyes? What kindness or courage hides in that face, what healing in those hands?

Opening ourselves to the presence of these strengths, we inhale our awareness of them, as in the breathing-through exercise. As our awareness grows, we feel our gratitude for them and an expansion of our experience.

Often we let our perceptions of the powers of others make us feel inadequate. Alongside an eloquent colleague, we can feel inarticulate; in the presence of a trained athlete, we can feel weak and clumsy; and we can come to resent both our self and the other person. In the light of the Great Ball of Merit, however, the gifts and good fortune of others appear not as competing challenges, but as resources we can honor and take pleasure in. We can learn to play detective, spying out treasures for the enhancement of life from even the unlikeliest material. Like air, and sun, and water, they form part of our common good.

In addition to releasing us from the mental cramp of envy, this spiritual practice offers two other rewards. One is pleasure in our own acuity as our merit-detecting ability improves. The second is the response of others who, though ignorant of the game we are playing, sense something in our manner that invites them to disclose more of the person they can be.

5. LEARNING TO SEE EACH OTHER

This practice is derived from the Buddhist practice of the Brahma-viharas, also known as the Four Immeasurables, which are loving-kindness, compassion, joy in the joy of others, and equanimity. Adapted for use in a social context, it helps us to see each other more truly and experience the depths of our interconnectedness.

In groups, I offer this as a guided meditation with par-ticipants sitting in pairs facing each other. Each serves as a "meditation object" for the other. At the close, I encourage them to proceed to use it, or any portion they like, as they go about their daily lives. It is an excellent antidote to boredom, when our eye falls on another person, say, on the subway or waiting in the checkout line. It charges that idle moment with beauty and discovery. It is also useful when dealing with people whom we are tempted to dislike or disregard; it breaks open our accustomed ways of viewing them. When used like this, as a meditation-in-action, one does not, of course, gaze long and deeply at the other, as in the guided exercise. A seemingly casual glance is enough. The guided group form goes like this:

> Sit in pairs, facing each other without speaking. Take in each other's presence as fully as you can. You may never see this person again: the opportunity to behold the uniqueness of this particular human being is given to you now. . . .
>
> As you behold this person, think of the powers that are there. . . . Open your awareness to the gifts and strengths and potential in this being. . . . Behind those eyes are unmeasured reserves of courage and intelligence . . . of creativity, endurance, wit, and wisdom. . . . There are gifts there, of which this person is not yet aware. . . . Consider what these powers could do for the healing of our planet, if they were believed and acted on. . . . As you consider that, feel your desire that this person be free from fear. . . . Experience how much you want this being to be free from fear, free from greed, released from hatred, and from sorrow and from the causes of suffering. . . . Know that what you are now experiencing is the great lovingkindness. . . .
>
> Now, sustaining your attention, open to the pain that is in this person's life. As in all human lives, there is suffering in this one. Though you can only guess at their forms, there are disappointments, failures, losses, loneliness, abuse. . . . there are hurts beyond the telling. . . . Let yourself open to that pain, to hurts that this person may never have told another being. . . . You cannot take those hurts away; you are not that powerful. But what you can do is be unafraid to be with them. As you let yourself simply be present with that suffering, know that what you are experiencing is the great compassion. It is very good for the healing of our world. . . .

*Now, with this person before you, consider how good it would
be to work together . . . on a joint project, toward a common
goal . . . to be taking risks together . . . conspiring together and
laughing together . . . celebrating the little successes along the
way, consoling each other over the setbacks, forgiving each other
when you make mistakes . . . and simply being there for each
other. . . . As you open to that possibility, what you open to is
the great wealth: the pleasure in each other's powers, the joy in
each other's joy. . . .*

*Lastly, let your awareness drop deeper within you, like a stone,
sinking below the level of what words can express, to the web
of relations that underlies all experience. It is the web of life in
which you have taken being . . . in which you are supported,
and interconnected through all space and time. . . . See the
being before you as if seeing the face of one who, at another
time, another place, was your lover or your enemy, your parent
or your child. . . . And now you meet again on this brink of
time. . . . And you know your lives are as intricately interwoven
as nerve cells in the mind of a great being. . . . Out of that vast
net you cannot fall. . . . No stupidity or failure or cowardice
can ever sever you from that living web. For that is what you
are . . . rest in that knowing. Rest in the Great Peace. . . .
Out of it we can act, we can dare anything . . . and let every
encounter be a homecoming to our true nature. . . . Indeed it
is so. . . .*

In doing this practice, we realize that we do not have to
be particularly noble or saint-like in order to wake up to the
power of our connection with other beings. In our time, that
simple awakening is the gift the global crises hold for us. For
all its horror and delusion, nuclear war, like the toxins that our

factories spew into our world, is also the manifestation of an awesome spiritual truth—the truth about the hell we create for ourselves when we cease to learn how to love. Saints, mystics, and prophets throughout the ages saw that law; now *all* can see it and none can escape its consequences. So we are caught now in a narrow place where we realize that Lao-tzu, the Buddha, Jesus, Muhammad, and our own hearts were right all along; and we are as scared and frantic as a cornered rat—and as dangerous. But if we let it, that narrow cul-de-sac can turn into a birth canal, pressing and pushing us through the darkness of pain, until we are delivered into . . . what? *Love* seems too weak a word. It is, as Paul said to the Romans, "the glory to be revealed in us." It stirs in us now.

For us to regard the threat of climate catastrophe, nuclear war, the dying seas, or the poisoned air as a monstrous injustice suggests that we never took seriously the injunction to love. Perhaps we thought all along that Gautama and Jesus were kidding or that their teachings were meant only for saints. But now comes the daunting revelation, that we are *all* called to be saints—not good necessarily, or pious, or devout—but saints in the sense of just caring for one another. One wonders what terrors this knowledge must hold that we fight it so and flee from it in such pain. Can our present capacity to extinguish all life tell us this? Can it force us to face the terrors of love? Can it be the occasion of our birth?

In that possibility we take heart. Even in confusion and fear, with all our weariness and petty faults, we can let that awareness work in and through our lives. Such simple practices as those offered here can help us do that, can help us begin to see our self and one another with fresh eyes.

Deep Time Practices

To help us perceive and use the opportunities the Great Turning brings us, we want to enlarge the timeframe in which we live our lives. We want to become more aware of our powerfully interwoven connections with past and future generations. These are both internal and reciprocal, refreshing the spirit and easing the tasks we feel called to take on. These practices have grown in variety and popularity over the last three decades. I will just share three of them here, and there are many more in *Coming Back to Life: The Work That Reconnects.*

6. THE BEINGS OF THE THREE TIMES

In workshops for activists, I often begin with an invocation of the beings of the three times. I invoke them because, on this brink of time, we need them to give us staying power.

> *We call first on the beings of the past:* **Be with us now**, *all you who have gone before. You, our ancestors and teachers, who walked and loved and faithfully tended this earth, be present to us now so that we may carry on the legacy you bequeathed us. Aloud and silently in our hearts, we say your names and see your faces. . . .*

> *Let us call on the beings of the present: All you with whom we live and work, all you with whom we live in this hard and dangerous time,* **be with us now**.

> *Let us come alive to our solidarity and know how deeply we belong to one another and to our Mother Earth. Let us open to our collective will and wisdom. Aloud and silently we say your names and picture your faces. . . .*

*Lastly, we call on the beings of the future: All you who will come after us on this Earth, **be with us now**. All you to be born in the ages to come, it is for your sakes, too, that we work to heal our world. We cannot picture your faces or say your names—you have none yet—but we feel the reality of your claim on life. Help us to be faithful to the work that must be done, so that there will be for you, as there was for our ancestors blue sky, fruitful land, clear waters.*

7. THE SEVENTH GENERATION

We have the ability, through our moral imagination, to break out of our temporal confine and let longer expanses of time become real to us. We can do it and even be good at it. This practice lets us experience ourselves as ancestors and see our lives through the eyes of future beings.

People sit facing each other in pairs oriented in the same directional axis, as in east-west or north-south. Those facing in one direction, say west, identify as their present-day self. Those facing them, in the opposite direction, say east, identify as a human of the seventh generation in the future. These roles are not interchangeable and are to be determined swiftly and clearly. Be sure all know what they're role they're playing.

Please grant two assumptions for the purpose of this ritual. The first assumption is that there will be humans living on Earth two hundred years from now. Even if you now think otherwise, please grant this assumption for the purpose of the ritual.

The second assumption is that the future ones have a cultural memory of what is happening in our time of the twenty-first century, whether it is carried by old documentaries or storytellers. This is an important assumption. It means humans are not all scattered in caves; to have a common culture, they must be living in life-sustaining communities—for the industrial growth society, already in decline, cannot last another two centuries.

In order for present and future beings to meet across two hundred years, we must go to a point outside of time. We travel there by the power of our intention and our moral imagination and by sounding together long and strong the seed syllable *AHH*, which stands for all that has not yet been spoken.

When the sounding has brought everyone to the point outside of time, explain the two roles as follows: You present-day people choose to see the person before you as a human of the seventh generation. And you future ones know that the person before you lives back in the year [today]. You have something to say to them and to ask: This will be spoken in my voice and taken as coming directly through your own heart-mind. You present-day ones will then answer out loud to the future ones who listen in silence. (Note that the word *ancestor* here refers to all people of preceding generations and is not limited to one's own genetic line.)

You as guide will speak for the future humans, three different times. Allow about three minutes for the present-day humans to respond to each inquiry. We encourage you to speak these three successive inquiries in your own words rather than reading them.

1. Ancestor, I greet you. It is so amazing to see your face, because all my life I have heard stories about the long ago time you are living. Some of the things I've heard I find hard to believe, so I'd like to check them out with you. They say that in your time there are a few people richer than the richest ancient kings, while billions of people are without enough food or shelter or clean water.

They tell us that in your time bombs are still being made that can destroy whole cities. We know about that, but they say you know about it too, right when the bombs are being made. They tell us that whole species of plants and animals are going extinct. We know about that too, because gone is gone. But they tell us that you know it too while it was happening. Is all this really true? And if it is, then what is it like for you to live in such a world?

Allow about three minutes for the present-day humans to respond. Then invite the future ones to silently acknowledge what they have heard, then to take their leave and walk to an empty place in front of another present-day being.

2. Ancestor, I greet you. When we in our generation find water we can drink and soil that's safe to grow food, it is thanks to the work you and your friends are doing on our behalf. It must be hard for you, especially at the beginning, standing up for beings you haven't met and will never meet. So I want to ask you these questions: What inspired you to start on this path? And what were the first steps you took?

Allow three minutes or so for the present-day humans to respond. And once again invite the future ones to acknowledge what they have heard, take their leave and move to a new place in front of yet another present-day being.

3. Ancestor, I greet you. We know you did not stop with those first steps. There are stories and songs about what you and your friends are doing to leave us a livable world. What they don't tell us, and what I would really like to know, is where you find the strength to do this. Where do you find the power to keep on going for the sake of life, despite all the obstacles and discouragements? Can you tell me?

After the present-day people have answered this third question, the future ones do not leave, but stay right there and respond to the next invitation.

Now, you of the Seventh Generation, it is your turn to talk. You have been listening to three ancestors speak of their experience of the Great Turning. As you listened, thoughts and feelings arose in you. Now is your chance to speak them. What is in your heart to say to the one before you? Very soon this person will be returning right into the midst of that darkness and danger. What words do you have for them?

Ask the present-day ones to just listen now, without speaking. Bring the ritual to a close by inviting the people in dyads to thank each other silently, and then to return to real time by once again sounding the seed syllable *AHH*.

And on the way back to real time, as we sound the AHH, you who spoke for the Seventh Generation can shake off that role. For the truth is, you belong to the Great Turning too.

With this particular practice, the processing can be almost as rewarding as the ritual itself, so it is useful to allow time for it. Ask for any reflections people would like to share with the whole group. Encourage those who speak up to identify the role they played.

8. CORBETT

The Buddha laid great emphasis on the intrinsic self-organizing power of intention. Even in an uncertain world, we can still choose where we put our minds and how we respond to circumstances and events. Justine and Michael Thomas describe the *genius of intention:* "When you are clear about your intention and at peace with yourself, aligned and moving with purpose in your work, then magic happens. People appear, affinity projects emerge, and support from unimagined quarters suddenly manifests."

In Corbett, our capacity for intention is tested and amplified by hearing from multiple perspectives:

1. the person who holds the intention
2. the voice of Doubt
3. the voice of a human ancestor
4. the voice of a future human

The practice was created near the small town of Corbett, Oregon, in the Columbia Gorge.

Method. People sit in groups of four. They are given moments of silence for each person to select an important intention they would like to explore further. Then each of the four takes a turn, first describing their intention, and then hearing it addressed from a different perspective by the other three people in the group. Going clockwise around the group, these perspectives are: the voice of Doubt, the voice of a human ancestor, and the voice of a future human.

Explain that each of these voices is meant to serve the person holding the intention. The voice of Doubt is helpful by bringing up misgivings and fears that could derail or weaken the intention if they are not face squarely. The ancestral voice brings in the wisdom of the past, and the future human opens vistas of what this intention could mean to coming generations.

Each person commenting gets about two minutes to speak while the intention holder listens silently. In this fashion, every person in the group gets a chance to speak all four voices.

Allow time at the end of each round for the intention holder to reflect on any insights that have arisen and to thank the other voices. Foursomes have found it helpful to assign each perspective to a chair and move to new seats before the next round.

Variations. Variation 1 is for each person to speak all four perspectives. In their turn, each intention holder first speaks their intention and then each of the other perspectives. This can be equally powerful and revelatory.

Variation 2 can be done in groups of three, in which case the fourth voice, that of the future, is spoken by the person who has spoken as Doubt. This can save time and often allows the voice of Doubt to speak more boldly, knowing there will be a chance to take a more encouraging role.

ACKNOWLEDGMENTS

What a blessing it has been to navigate this time, which has been very trying for our world, with an undertaking so meaningful and reassuring. It was good to have such a compelling lens for illuminating the root insights in my original writing. In the midst of the pandemic, the spreading fires and smoke, the police brutality and systemic injustice, and the dramatically contested election—these intense challenges were new illustrations of the essential insights of the earlier editions of this book and more relevant than ever now. In the acceleration of the Great Unraveling, the very difficulties of our world reaffirmed our commitment to the project. I offer here my gratitude for so many people who made this much-loved book possible.

At Parallax Press, Arnie Kotler first conceived of the idea and committed the newly organized publishing house to this project in 1990. His love for the work and support for this collection were foundational in the beginning. Rachel Neuman urged me to bring out a second edition in 2007 and served as senior editor; I am grateful to her and also Aryeh Shell for their editorial assistance. Hisae Matsuda came to me with her conviction that a third and updated edition would be meaningful and helpful in these troubled times. Her commitment and vision helped make this a stronger book, relevant to the young activists of today. I also thank Katie Eberle at Parallax for cover and interior design and other Parallax staff for making this edition possible.

For material support, I am ever grateful to Christopher Hormel for his generous funding; his belief in the project made it possible to carry out this work under the logistical challenges of editing and collaboration during the pandemic. I also thank the Kalliopeia Foundation for ongoing support for my work across these recent years; it is deeply affirming. In fall 2020, Broadfork Farm hosted me for a three-week writing retreat; the promise and nobility of that land in Trout Lake, Washington, is in these pages. My thanks to Kaye Jones and Adam Hyde and Rye, Fisher, and Archer for helping me stay in touch with the ongoing life of the farm, evoking future generations of lovers, farmers, and compost enthusiasts.

Many close friends and family were instrumental in completing this anniversary edition. My Seven Sisters dharma group, as well as Linda Seeley and Anne Symens-Bucher, provided day-to-day support, all of them glad that I was bringing forth something that was so meaningful for me and so expressive of my love for the world. With Sean Kelly, a key thinking partner, we kept each other company, looking over the edge of the world at scenarios of collapse and renewal. Much gratitude to my *beau fils* Gregoire Vion and grandson Julien Vion for technical help in laptop communications and editing. To my son Christopher, my gratitude for widening my understanding of the divergent views in our country. To my son Jack, thank you for always calling me to deepen my thinking, as well as for your canny appreciation of the work I do. I am ever inspired by the activism of your daughters, my granddaughters Eliza and Lydia, as well as of their mother, my *belle fille* Charlotte. To my daughter Peggy, thank you for your vigilant care of my health, and for being, with your wit and warmth, so much like your namesake, my

Mama. And deep gratitude to my husband, Fran, for the support and respect he gave the Work That Reconnects and my teaching over three decades. Even now his companionship fills these pages with great warmth of heart.

This book greatly benefited from the sharp eyes and feedback from several thoughtful readers. To Catherine Johnson, thank you for taking a break from your election postcard writing to bring your clarity, humor, and wordsmithing to several key chapters. To Wendy Johnson, thank you for your many excellent suggestions and your devotion to the Buddhadharma that informed your response. I felt you right by my side, with flower and gift offerings through the months. Kaye Jones, a key member of the team, accompanied me through the many phases of book development and completion, with her own true eye and unique perspective on the work. Our team of three—Kaye, Stephanie, and I—was forged as we worked together on *A Wild Love for the World*; it has been a joy and blessing, at times a magical dynamic, as our three generations offered depth to our work.

To my editor, Stephanie Kaza—this book would not have happened without you. In every step of the way, you carried this with such determination, care, and insistence on the best quality writing and scholarly excellence. I felt you at my back throughout the entire process. I never could have done this without you; you were so patient throughout our many zoom editing sessions. You held the unwavering conviction that this work was well worth doing for all those readers to come.

And so much gratitude for my own dear old body-mind in its ninety-second year. It stuck with me through the pandemic, the election, and through completion of new writing as well as significant updating and editing of this manuscript. The project was fueled by a great sense of delight, with so much gratitude for Kaye and Stephanie, and for the work itself. As I reread and rethought the foundations of my work, I fell in love with our world over and over again.

Throughout this undertaking, I have felt renewed gratitude and respect for the Buddhadharma and for the many teachers who transmitted and shared it generously with me. Over all these years, the Dharma to me is, as Buddhaghosa described, like a tough and verdant vine—beautiful wherever you pick it up—beautiful at the roots, beautiful in the tendrils, beautiful in the flowers. All of this feeds my ever-increasing wonder and reverence for the great teacher, Gautama the Buddha, and all who have followed in his footsteps. May these teachings illumine for us the way ahead.

FOR FURTHER STUDY
JOANNA MACY LIFE TIMELINE

For further details, see Joanna Macy, *Widening Circles: A Memoir* (2000).

May 2, 1929. Mary Joanna Rogers born in Los Angeles, California, to Margaret Kinsey and Hartley Rogers of Buffalo, New York.

1934. Joanna's parents move back to New York State with her and her older brother, Hartley Jr., and younger brother, John.

1938–1946. Joanna and her family live in Manhattan in a series of apartments; Joanna attends Lycée Français de New York through the first baccalaureate; she and her brothers spend summers at their grandparents' farm near Albion, New York.

1950. B.A. degree after four years at Wellesley College, with a major in religion and minor in political science.

1950. On a Fulbright Scholarship at the Institute D'études Politiques in Bordeaux, France, where she prepares a report on the French Communist Party.

1952–1954. Recruited by the Central Intelligence Agency (CIA) for its first Career Officer Training Program in Washington, DC.

May 1953. Marriage to Francis Underhill Macy, whose graduate studies at Harvard University and government service focus on the Soviet Union.

1954. Fran accepts a radio broadcasting job, and the family moves from Washington, DC, to New York. First son, Christopher, born.

1956–1960. Family moves to Munich, Germany, where Fran serves as deputy program director for Radio Liberty, broadcasting to the seventeen nations of the Soviet Union; Joanna learns German, skis in the nearby Alps, and discovers poet Rainer Maria Rilke. Second son, John (Jack), born in Munich in 1957.

1960–1964. Macy family in Washington, DC: Fran oversees the Russian desk of Voice of America; Joanna works half-time with the State Department Office of the Chief Protocol serving African diplomats. Home on Lowell Street becomes family base for the next twenty-five years. Daughter Margaret (Peggy) born in 1961.

1964–1969. Family lives in India, Tunisia, and Nigeria as Fran runs Peace Corps country programs. In India, Joanna works with Tibetan monks and lamas fleeing Tibet and, through them, begins her journey with Buddhism that will guide the rest of her life.

1969–1972. Back in their Washington, DC, home, Fran works as Peace Corps director for Africa, and Joanna works half-time as speechwriter for the director of the Greater Washington Urban League, focused on civil rights, and teaches world religions classes at two private high schools.

1972–1977. Family moves to Syracuse, New York; Joanna begins her PhD at Syracuse University in religious studies with a focus on Buddhism; Fran creates the Regional Learning Service for adults seeking to complete high school and college degrees. In 1972 Fran survives a major heart attack. In 1974 Joanna takes refuge vows with Karma Khechog Palmo (Freda Bedi), who is preparing His Holiness the Karmapa's first visit to North America. Macy family renovates an inner-city house, inviting others to live with them in a cooperative household.

1976. Joanna returns on her own to India for the first of many times and is reunited with her Tibetan friends at their new home of Tashi Jong. Makes her first visit to Sri Lanka.

May 1977. Joanna and Peggy meet up with Jack at Tufts University in Boston and attend the Cousteau Society symposium on the environment, a turning point in her life.

May 1978. Joanna defends her doctoral dissertation, "Mutual Causality in Buddhism and General Systems Theory," and receives her PhD, with high distinction.

May 1979. First article on despair work published in *New Age Journal* with record-breaking reader response. Leaves for a year of fieldwork in Sri Lanka as participant observer with the Sarvodaya Shramadana movement.

1980. At the end of her year of fieldwork, Joanna is deported from Sri Lanka after her nonviolence work with Tamil people. That summer, in California she leads her first public despair workshop, thinking it a brief diversion on the way to an academic position, but the workshops continue nonstop for the next forty years. Interhelp organization emerges to promote despair work; publishes *Evolutionary Blues* journal; holds annual national conferences and workshops.

1982–1987. Teaching tours of the United Kingdom, Germany, and Japan, where in each country the work blossoms. *Despair and Personal Power in the Nuclear Age* is published in 1983, with a German translation in 1985, before a major tour in Germany. Five-week Australian tour in 1985; meets Australian activist John Seed; cocreates the Council of All Beings. Despair Work is renamed as Deep Ecology work, and *Thinking Like a Mountain* is published in 1988.

Lives in various places in the San Francisco Bay area 1982 to 1985 while Fran serves as director for the Association of Humanistic Psychology and begins leading delegations to the

Soviet Union drawing on Deep Ecology work and facilitated by Interhelp activists. *Dharma and Development* is published in 1983 and is expanded in 1985 to include the Sri Lankan civil war. **1991–1993.** In 1991 her dissertation, *Mutual Causality in Buddhism and General Systems Theory*, is published, as well as the first edition of *World as Lover, World as Self*. In 1993 Joanna is laid up with pneumonia and begins translating Rilke poems with Anita Barrows, which, over the next twenty-seven years, yields four published books and much joy (*Rilke's Book of Hours, A Year with Rilke, In Praise of Mortality: Selections from the Duino Elegies and Sonnets to Orpheus*, and *Letters to a Young Poet*).

1987–2009. In 1987, Joanna and Fran buy their first house in Berkeley, California, and travel with Peggy to Tibet. Graduate teaching at the California Institute for Integral Studies, John F. Kennedy University, Starr King School for the Ministry, University of Creation Spirituality, and Schumacher College in Devon, United Kingdom.

Starts study action group on nuclear waste and develops the Nuclear Guardianship Project, which leads to her deep time work and Fran's founding of the Center for Safe Energy in the former Soviet Union. Teaching tours around the world, both on her own and with Fran, with Deep Ecology Institutes 1991–1994 in the US and Canada, intensives at Findhorn, and multiple workshop tours in Europe and Russia.

In 1995, Joanna and Fran, along with daughter Peggy and her husband, move into a duplex home in Berkeley. In 1998 the seminal teaching manual, *Coming Back to Life: Practices to Reconnect Our Lives, Our World*, is published with coauthor Molly Young Brown. *Widening Circle: A Memoir* is published in 2000. A second edition of *World as Lover, World as Self* is published in 2007.

January 20, 2009. Fran Macy dies at home of a heart attack and is well honored by friends and family around the world.

2009–present. Joanna remains in her sunny upstairs flat in Berkeley, living near her children and three grandchildren. Offers multiple global seminars on climate change, deep adaptation, the Work That Reconnects. Publishes *Active Hope: How to Face the Mess We're in without Going Crazy* with British collaborator Chris Johnstone in 2012.

Major teaching tours in 2013 to the United Kingdom and Germany. Leads weeklong residentials at Spirit Rock Meditation Center. Receives Bioneers Lifetime Contribution Award in 2013. A second and expanded edition of *Coming Back to Life: The Updated Guide to the Work That Reconnects* is published in 2014. The Joanna Macy Center is founded at Naropa University in 2015.

In 2020, *A Wild Love for the World: Joanna Macy and the Work of Our Time*, with editor Stephanie Kaza, is released on Joanna's ninetieth birthday. The American Academy of Religion gives a scholarly tribute to Joanna and her global legacy. With coauthors and editor collaborators, she prepares a second edition of *Active Hope*, a new translation of Rilke's *Letters to a Young Poet*, and a third edition of *World as Lover, World as Self*, all for 2021 publication.

A BUDDHIST GLOSSARY

abhaya mudra. Sanskrit. A raised right hand, the fear-not gesture encountered in some Buddhist and Hindu sacred imagery.

akasa. Sanskrit. The infinite expanse of space.

ananta. Sanskrit. Endless.

anatta Pali. No-self. Sanskrit: *anatman.*

atman. Sanskrit. An eternal, universal Self at the core of one's being.

ayatana. Sanskrit. The sphere or gateway through which perception occurs.

bardo. Tibetan. A transitional or liminal state between death and rebirth.

bhikkhu. Pali (plural *bhikkhus*). A monk. Sanskrit: *bhikshu.*

bhikkhuni. Pali (plural *bhikkhunis*). A nun. Sanskrit: *bhikshuni.*

bodhicitta. Sanskrit. The intention to serve the welfare of all beings, the mind of love.

bodhisattva. Sanskrit. A being who, in their great compassion, delays entry into nirvana in order to address the world's suffering. Pali: *bodhisatta.*

brahmavihara. Sanskrit. The Four Brahmaviharas, or Four Immeasurables, are known as the Four Abodes of the Buddha. The Four Abodes are lovingkindness, *maitri* (Sanskrit) or *metta* (Pali); compassion, *karuna* (both Pali and Sanskrit); joy in the joy of others, *mudita* (both Pali and Sanskrit); and equanimity, *upeksha* (Sanskrit) or *upekkha* (Pali).

Buddhadharma. The teachings of the Buddha, the teachings of awakening and liberation.

dana. Pali and Sanskrit. Generosity.

*dhamma*s (Pali) or *dharma*s (Sanskrit). Series of events or units of experience.

Dharma Chakra. Sanskrit. The wheel of Dharma.

dukkha (Pali) or *duhkha* (Sanskrit). The truth of suffering.

ehi passiko. Pali. "Come and see," words of the Buddha exhorting students to test and experience the teachings.

Four Noble Truths. (Pali terms used here.) Comprising *dukkha* (suffering, an innate feature of existence); *samudaya* (origin, arising) of this dukkha, which arises or "comes together" with *tanha* (craving, desire, or attachment); *nirodha* (cessation, ending) of this dukkha can be attained by the letting go of this tanha; *magga* (path, the Noble Eightfold Path) is the path leading to renouncement of tanha and cessation of dukkha.

kalyanamitra. Sanskrit. Spiritual friendship.

karma. Sanskrit. Literally, action, but also frequently understood to mean the fruit or consequences of past actions. Pali: *kamma.*

karuna. Pali and Sanskrit. Compassion.

koan. Japanese. Words used by Zen masters to test and train their students.

magga. Pali. The path leading to cessation of suffering; literally, the path. Sanskrit: *marga.*

mamatta. Pali. "Mineness," the sense of selfishness and egoism.

manomaya. Pali and Sanskrit. "Mind-made."

maya. Sanskrit. material manifestation, ultimately illusory due to its impermanence.

metta. Pali. Lovingkindness. Sanskrit: *maitri.*

moksha. Sanskrit. Spirit and release, liberation.

mudita. Pali and Sanskrit. Joy in the joy of others, sympathetic joy.

nirodha, Pali and Sanskrit. The truth of the cessation of suffering; the third Noble Truth taught by the Buddha.

nirvana. Sanskrit. Liberation. Pali: *nibbana.*

paramita. Sanskrit. "Gone beyond" or to the "other side," as well as "perfection." Pali: *parami.*

paticca samuppada. Pali. The interdependent co-arising of all things. Sanskrit: *pratityasamutpada.*

prajna. Sanskrit. Wisdom.

Prajnaparamita. Perfection of Wisdom, Mother of All Buddhas.

prakrti. Sanskrit. Nature principle.

samsara. Sanskrit. The world; the cycle of birth, death, and reincarnation.

samudaya. Pali. The truth about the cause of our suffering; the second Noble Truth.

sangha. Sanskrit. A monastic community or a community of spiritual friends; the third of the Three Refuges in Buddhism.

sankhara. Pali. Volitional formations in Pali language. Sanskrit: *samskara.*

Sariputra. *Sariputra.* The Buddha's most learned disciple.

satyagraha. Sanskrit. Truth-force, holding firmly to truth. The name of the form of nonviolent civil resistance coined and practiced by Gandhi.

shakti. Sanskrit. Energy, power, the feminine principle.

Shantideva. Beloved and highly influential saint of the eighth century.

shramadana. Giving (*dana*) of human energy (*shrama*).

Siddhartha Gautama. The historical Buddha.

sila. Pali. Moral action.

sunya. Sanskrit. Empty or zero.

sunyata. Sanskrit. Emptiness. Often refers to the "no-self" of *anatman* or *anatta.* Pali: *sunnata.*

sutra. Sanskrit. Literally, a string or thread; collected teachings strung together like beads on a string. (Pali): *sutta.*

tat tvam asi. Sanskrit. "That art thou"; you are that.

tathata. Pali. "Thatness" or "suchness."

tonglen. Tibetan. Literally, "giving and taking." *Tong* means "giving or sending," and *len* means "receiving or taking." Refers to a meditation practice in Tibetan Buddhism, in which practitioners give and take energy and cultivate compassion and empathy.

upaya. Sanskrit. Skill in means, or skillful means.

upekkha. Pali. Equanimity. Sanskrit: *upeksha.*

vipassana. Pali. Insight meditation, a form of meditation that seeks insight into the true nature of reality. Sanskrit: vipashyana.

viriya. Pali. Courage, energy, diligence. Sanskrit: *virya.*

yab-yum. Tibetan. Mother-father embrace, a symbol of the union of wisdom and compassion, depicted as male and female deities.

yathabutham. Pali. Reality as it is.

NOTES

1. WORLD AS LOVER, WORLD AS SELF

1. Andrew Harvey, *The Return of the Mother* (New Zealand: Penguin, 2004).
2. Italo Calvino, *Cosmicomics* (New York: Harcourt Brace Jovanovich, 1968), 43–47.
3. Ibid.
4. Ibid.
5. Natachee Scott Momaday, http://www.poemhunter.com/i/ebooks/pdf/natachee_scott_momaday_2004_9.pdf.
6. Thich Nhat Hanh, *Call Me by My True Names: The Collected Poems* (Berkeley: Parallax Press, 1992).

2. GROUNDING IN GRATITUDE

1. This translation of the Mohawk version of the Haudenosaunee Thanksgiving Address was developed, published in 1993, and provided, courtesy of: Six Nations Indian Museum and the Tracking Project. All rights reserved. Thanksgiving Address: Greetings to the Natural World English version: John Stokes and Kanawahienton (David Benedict, Turtle Clan/Mohawk) Mohawk version: Rokwaho (Dan Thompson, Wolf Clan/Mohawk) Original inspiration: Tekaronianekon (Jake Swamp, Wolf Clan/Mohawk). https://howtoliveonpurpose.com/tag/jake-swamp.

3. THE GATEWAY TO DESPAIR

1. Kazimierz Dabrowski, *Positive Disintegration* (Boston: Little Brown, 1964).
2. Norbert Wiener, *Human Use of Human Beings: Cybernetics and Society* (New York: Avon Books, 1967).
3. Thich Nhat Hanh, "The Bells of Mindfulness," in *Spiritual Ecology: The Cry of the Earth*, ed. Llewellyn Vaughan-Lee (Point Reyes, CA: The Golden Sufi Center, 2013).

4. For more information on John Seed, see John Seed, Joanna Macy, Pat Fleming, and Arne Naess, *Thinking Like a Mountain: Towards a Council of All Beings* (Philadelphia: New Society, 1988).
5. Rev. angel Kyodo williams, in *Radical Dharma: Talking Race, Love, and Liberation*, Rev. angel Kyodo williams, Lama Rod Owens, and Jasmine Syedullah (Berkeley, CA: North Atlantic Books, 2016).

5. THE WHEEL OF INTERBEING

1. *Digha Nikaya* II.33.
2. *Samyutta Nikaya* II.28, 65 *Majjhima Nikaya* II.32, etc.
3. *Samyutta Nikaya* II.103, 113.
4. *Digha Nikaya* II.1.
5. Sangharakshita, *The Complete Works* (Cambridge, UK: Windhorse Publications, 2019).
6. Ervin Laszlo, *Introduction to Systems Philosophy: Towards a New Paradigm of Contemporary Thought* (New York: Harper, 1973), 293.
7. Ibid., 170.

6. THE CO-ARISING OF KNOWER AND KNOWN

1. Part 3, chapter 7, verse 16; English translation by Swami Nikhilananda, from https://www.sankaracharya.org/brihadaranyaka_upanishad.php.
2. *Majjhima Nikaya* 1.259-60.
3. Ibid., I.257.
4. *Samyutta Nikaya* III. 57.
5. *Anguttara Nikaya* II.24.

7. KARMA: THE CO-ARISING OF DOER AND DEED

1. *Samyutta Nikaya* II.26.
2. T. W. Rhys Davids, *Dialogues of the Buddha (Digha Nikaya)* (London: Pali Text Society, 1973) II, 189.
3. H. Oldenburg, *Buddha: His Life, His Doctrine, His Order* (Delhi: Indological Book House, 1971), 243.
4. *Anguttara Nikaya* I.174.
5. *Samyutta Nikaya* 11.38.
6. *Majjhima Nikaya* 1.32.
7. *Samyutta Nikaya* II. 264.
8. Karl W. Deutsch, "Toward a Cybernetic Model of Man and Society," in Walter Buckley, ed., *Modern Systems Research for the Behavioral Scientist* (Chicago: Aldine, 1968) 397.
9. Ibid., 398.

10. Ibid., 398–99.

11. O. H. Mowrer, "Ego Psychology, Cybernetics, and Learning Theory," in *Modern Systems Research for the Behavioral Scientist: A Sourcebook*, ed. Walter Buckley (Chicago: Aldine, 1968), 338.

8. THE CO-ARISING OF SELF AND SOCIETY

1. Digha Nikaya I.99.
2. Ibid., II.77.
3. Ibid., I.135.
4. Lucien Stryk, ed., *World of the Buddha: A Reader* (New York: Doubleday Anchor, 1968), 245. The Seventh Pillar Edicts of Asoka.
5. P. Wheelwright, ed. and tr., *Aristotle: Natural Science, Psychology, and Nicomachean Ethics* (New York: Odyssey, 1935), 35.
6. Vinaya, I.113.

9. MOTHER OF ALL BUDDHAS

1. All quotes from Edward Conze, trans., *The Perfection of Wisdom: Eight Thousand Lines and Its Verse Summary* (San Francisco: Four Seasons Foundation, 1973).
2. Ibid., chap. 12, verses 253–57.
3. Ibid., chap. 18, on Emptiness (RiBa).
4. Ibid., verse 141, The Praise of Perfect Wisdom.
5. Ibid., verse 144.
6. Ibid., verse 141.
7. A. K. Coomaraswamy, "Kha and Other Words Denoting Zero in Connection with the Metaphysics of Space," *Bulletin of the School of Oriental Studies*, London Institution, 7, no. 3 (1934): 496.
8. D. T. Suzuki, "Emptiness," in *On Indian Mahayana Buddhism*, ed. Edward Conze (New York: Harper Torch Books, 1968).
9. Richard Lannoy, *The Speaking Tree: A Study of Indian Culture and Society* (Oxford: Oxford University Press, 1971), 107.

11. THE GREENING OF THE SELF

1. Robert N. Bellah, Richard Madsen, William M. Sullivan, Ann Swidler, and Steven M. Tipton. *Habits of the Heart: Individualism and Commitment in American Life* (Berkeley: University of California Press, 1985).
2. Gregory Bateson. *Steps to an Ecology of Mind* (New York: Ballantine Books, 1972).

3. Ibid.
4. Arne Naess, "Self-Realization," in *Thinking Like a Mountain: Towards a Council of All Beings*, ed. by John Seed, Joanna Macy, Pat Fleming, and Arne Naess (Philadelphia: New Society, 1988).

12. FAITH, POWER, AND DEEP ECOLOGY

1. Justin Kenrick, personal communication, 1985. For his current work, see https://www.resilience.org/resilience-author/justin-kenrick.
2. Paul Shepard, with Daniel McKinley, *Subversive Science: Essays Toward An Ecology of Man* (Boston: Houghton Mifflin, 1969).
3. John Seed, Joanna Macy, Pat Fleming, and Arne Naess, *Thinking Like a Mountain: Towards a Council of All Beings* (Philadelphia: New Society, 1988).

13. IN LEAGUE WITH THE BEINGS OF THE FUTURE

1. The Indigenous Environmental Network, www.ienearth.org.
2. Walter Bresette, Anishinaabe Nation, www.protecttheearth.net.
3. Joanna Macy, *Prayers for a Thousand Years*, ed. Elizabeth Roberts and Elias Amidon (San Francisco: Harper Collins, 1999).

14. THE FULLNESS OF TIME

1. Tyrone Cashman, unpublished manuscript, 1989.
2. Robert J. Lifton. *The Broken Connection: On Death and the Continuity of Life* (New York: Simon and Schuster, 1979), 338.
3. Ibid.
4. Larry Dossey, *Space, Time, and Medicine* (Boulder, CO: Shambhala, 1982), 49.
5. Rainer Maria Rilke, *Rilke's Book of Hours: Love Poems to God*, trans. Anita Barrows and Joanna Macy (New York: Riverhead Books, 1996), 51.
6. Well-Being of Future Generations Act 2015, https://www.futuregenerations.wales/about-us/future-generations-act.

15. THE GREAT TURNING

1. For more on William Ruckelshaus's long and esteemed career, including his years with the Environmental Protection Agency, see https://en.wikipedia.org/wiki/William_Ruckelshaus, and this remembrance, https://ruckelshauscenter.wsu.edu/remembering-bill.

2. For current writing from James Gustave Speth, see his latest book, with Peter Denton, *Imagine a Joyful Economy* (Kelowna, BC: Wood Lake Books, 2020).

3. Ludwig Feuerbach, *The Essence of Christianity* (London: Trübner, 1881).

16. COLLECTIVE INTELLIGENCE: THE HOLONIC SHIFT

1. Arthur Koestler, *The Ghost in the Machine* (London: Penguin, 1990), original 1967. For more on holons, see https://panarchy.org/koestler/holon.1969.html.

CREDITS

ENTERING THE BARDO

Posted at Emergence Magazine, 2020, https://emergencemagazine
.org/story/entering-the-bardo.

1. WORLD AS LOVER, WORLD AS SELF

Originally adapted from the Viriditas Lecture on Spiritual Values
and Contemporary Issues, Friends of Creation Spirituality,
November 1987, Berkeley, California.

2. GROUNDING IN GRATITUDE

First published in *World as Lover, World as Self* (Berkeley, CA:
Parallax Press, 2007), 75–86.

3. THE GATEWAY OF DESPAIR

Based on the original booklet *Despairwork* (Philadelphia: New
Society Publishers, 1981), with additions and adaptation from
other despair writing.

4. WISDOM AND ACTION

Adapted from "Indra's Net," *The Ten Directions*, Zen Center Los
Angeles, December 1982, 7–11.

5. THE WHEEL OF INTERBEING

Adapted from chapters 6 and 8, *Mutual Causality in Buddhism and
General Systems Theory* (Albany, NY: SUNY Press, 1991), 107–16,
141–59.

6. THE CO-ARISING OF KNOWER AND KNOWN

Adapted from chapter 7, *Mutual Causality in Buddhism and General
Systems Theory* (Albany, NY: SUNY Press, 1991), 117–39.

7. KARMA: THE CO-ARISING OF DOER AND DEED

Adapted from chapter 9, *Mutual Causality in Buddhism and General Systems Theory* (Albany, NY: SUNY Press, 1991), 161–81.

8. THE CO-ARISING OF SELF AND SOCIETY

Adapted from chapter 10, *Mutual Causality in Buddhism and General Systems Theory* (Albany, NY: SUNY Press, 1991), 183–92.

9. MOTHER OF ALL BUDDHAS

Adapted from "Perfection of Wisdom: Mother of All Buddhas," in *Beyond Androcentrism: New Essays on Women and Religion*, ed. Rita M. Gross (Missoula, MT: Scholars Press for the American Academy of Religion, 1977), and articles by the same title in *Anima Magazine* (Fall 1986) and *Inquiring Mind* 17, no. 1 (2001): 28–29.

10. OPENINGS

First half adapted from *Widening Circles: A Memoir* (Gabriola Island, BC: New Society Publishers, 2000), 2–3.

11. THE GREENING OF THE SELF

First published in *Dharma Gaia* (Berkeley, CA: Parallax Press, 1989), 53–63.

12. FAITH, POWER, AND DEEP ECOLOGY

Adapted from a lecture at Schumacher College, Bristol, England, October 1986.

13. IN LEAGUE WITH THE BEINGS OF THE FUTURE

Adapted from the original version in *Creation* magazine, 1989.

14. THE FULLNESS OF TIME

Adapted from a presentation at the Conference on the Post-Modern Presidency, Santa Barbara, CA, July 1989, and further developed for this edition.

15. THE GREAT TURNING

Adapted from "The Great Turning as Compass and Lens," *YES: A Journal of Positive Futures* (Spring 2000), and "The Great Turning," in *World as Lover, World as Self* (Berkeley, CA: Parallax Press, 2007), 139–47.

16. COLLECTIVE INTELLIGENCE: THE HOLONIC SHIFT

Adapted from "Collective Self-Interest: The Holonic Shift," *World Business Academy Perspectives* 9, no.1 (1995): 19–22, and Liz Campbell, "Interview with Joanna Macy," *Association for Humanistic Psychology Newsletter* (July/August 1982): 15–18.

17. SHAMBHALA WARRIORS: A PROPHECY

First published in *World as Lover, World as Self* (Berkeley, CA: Parallax Press, 1991).

18. COURAGE FOR THE ROAD

Adapted and expanded from "Learning to See in the Dark amid Catastrophe: An Interview with Deep Ecologist Joanna Macy." Dahr Jamail, Truthout, February 13, 2017.

ABOUT JOANNA MACY

Joanna Macy, PhD, teacher and author, is a scholar of Buddhism, systems thinking, and deep ecology. Interweaving her scholarship with four decades of activism, her wide-ranging work addresses psychological and spiritual issues of the nuclear age, the cultivation of ecological awareness, and the fruitful resonance between Buddhist thought and contemporary science. Her group methods have been adopted and adapted widely in classrooms, churches, and grassroots organizing work. Her work helps people transform despair and apathy in the face of overwhelming social and ecological crises into constructive, collaborative action. As the root teacher of the Work That Reconnects, Macy has created a groundbreaking framework for personal and social change of seeing the world as our larger body. Macy's work on the Great Turning envisions a post-empire, post-corporate future for humanity based in sustainable, just, and caring communities. A much-loved translator (with Anita Barrows) of the poems of Rainer Maria Rilke, Macy infuses poetry into the tough work of social activism in her own writing. Her most recent books are a second edition of *Active Hope: How to Face the Mess We're in without Going Crazy* (with Chris Johnstone) and *A Wild Love for the World* (edited by Stephanie Kaza). She continues to write and teach in Berkeley, California.

Monastics and visitors practice the art of mindful living in the tradition of Thich Nhat Hanh at our mindfulness practice centers around the world. To reach any of these communities, or for information about how individuals, couples, and families can join in a retreat, please contact:

PLUM VILLAGE
33580 Dieulivol, France
plumvillage.org

MAGNOLIA GROVE MONASTERY
Batesville, MS 38606, USA
magnoliagrovemonastery.org

BLUE CLIFF MONASTERY
Pine Bush, NY 12566, USA
bluecliffmonastery.org

DEER PARK MONASTERY
Escondido, CA 92026, USA
deerparkmonastery.org

EUROPEAN INSTITUTE OF
APPLIED BUDDHISM
D-51545 Waldbröl, Germany
eiab.eu

THAILAND PLUM VILLAGE
Nakhon Ratchasima
30130 Thailand
thaiplumvillage.org

ASIAN INSTITUTE OF
APPLIED BUDDHISM
Lantau Island, Hong Kong
pvfhk.org

LA MAISON DE L'INSPIR
77510 Verdelot, France
maisondelinspir.org

HEALING SPRING MONASTERY
77510 Verdelot, France
healingspringmonastery.org

STREAM ENTERING
MONASTERY
Beaufort, Victoria 3373, Australia
nhapluu.org

The Mindfulness Bell, a journal of the art of mindful living in the tradition of Thich Nhat Hanh, is published three times a year by our community. To subscribe or to see the worldwide directory of Sanghas, or local mindfulness groups, visit mindfulnessbell.org.

PARALLAX PRESS, a nonprofit publisher founded by Zen Master Thich Nhat Hanh, publishes books and media on the art of mindful living and Engaged Buddhism. We are committed to offering teachings that help transform suffering and injustice. Our aspiration is to contribute to collective insight and awakening, bringing about a more joyful, healthy, and compassionate society.

View our entire library at parallax.org.